John Affleck Bridges

Poets All

John Affleck Bridges

Poets All

ISBN/EAN: 9783337778224

Printed in Europe, USA, Canada, Australia, Japan

Cover: Foto ©Thomas Meinert / pixelio.de

More available books at **www.hansebooks.com**

POETS ALL

BY

JOHN A. BRIDGES

AUTHOR OF

"IDYLLS OF A LOST VILLAGE," "A BRUMMAGEM BARON,"
"WET DAYS," ETC.

"Scribimus indocti doctique poemata."—HOR.
"Both the wise and the witless scribble."—PRAED.

London
WARD AND DOWNEY
12 YORK STREET, COVENT GARDEN
1893

CONTENTS.

CHAP.		PAGE
I.	THE POET AT HOME	1
II.	A KINDLY CRITIC	9
III.	A COUNTRY SQUIRE	20
IV.	MAGGIE ELLIS ...	29
V.	THE COMING GUESTS ...	36
VI.	THE DESCENT OF THE IMMORTALS ...	47
VII.	THE NEW 'STUDY'	56
VIII.	THE PURSUIT OF 'COPY' ...	67
IX.	A CRITICAL DISCUSSION	84
X.	THE RECTOR ON POETS AND POETRY	96
XI.	AN INTERRUPTED COMPETITION	110
XII.	AT THE HOME FARM	127
XIII.	THE YOUNG SCHOOL-MASTER	138
XIV.	THE RECTOR'S GLASS-HOUSE ...	148
XV.	THE DAWN OF AMBITION	162
XVI.	DEFERRED WOOINGS ...	171
XVII.	MAGGIE MAKES A DISCOVERY	182
XVIII.	WHAT BECAME OF THE ROSE	195

CONTENTS.

CHAP.		PAGE
XIX.	THE CRITIC'S THUMB ...	201
XX.	A SYMPATHIZING PUBLISHER	213
XXI.	A GLIMPSE OF FAME ...	226
XXII.	THE KING IS DEAD ...	238
XXIII.	THE CRITIC IS MAGNANIMOUS	254
XXIV.	LONG LIVE THE KING	261
XXV.	MAGGIE IS WITNESS TO A LOVE SCENE ...	270
XXVI.	A SEASIDE WALK	278
XXVII.	A LAUREATE SPOILED	289

POETS ALL.

CHAPTER I.

THE POET AT HOME.

"*POETS ALL!* What an absurd name!" exclaims an intending reader, hastily throwing aside the book and choosing instead another with, at first sight, a more sensible and intelligible title—which does not necessarily guarantee a more sensible or intelligible interior.

And why not *Poets All*, I should like to ask? Surely if Horace, before the stylus was superseded by the gold pen, and the waxen tablets by foolscap—ill-omened word!—could assert (perhaps with a little of his poetical licence) that every one, learned or ignorant, was writing poetry, the remark must have far more truth in our own time. It may indeed in the present day be shown—with the usual exceptions,

B

to include the above-mentioned intending reader—to be almost literally true.

It is of course a well-known fact that almost every one, from Prime Minister to the lowest of those for whom he caters, loves the elusive pursuit of rhymes. True that rhymes are not always, or often, poetry. But as some of the compositions that have been discovered on the walls of convicts' cells have not been entirely wanting in the divine *afflatus*, it is hard to see whose claims can be called in question.

Poets are of so many sorts. Some few have, implanted in their breasts, a genuine poetical feeling, which they have also the power of expressing. Others have the feeling without the power—sometimes without even the wish—to give utterance to it. Some, and these by far the largest portion, resemble machines in their capacity for assimilating any raw material which seems likely to yield the necessary staple. Bees wander far afield in search of honey, and some bees are so clever as to extract it from the most unpromising flowers. If these last, however, did not contain honey the cleverest bee would have to return empty to the hive. So likewise would the poets who are dependent upon others for their raw material. There must be poetry one would think in those from whom the poetical-honey-gatherers accumulate their vast stores. In these days of eager competition I notice that few people, however stolid their appearance, escape rifling. Who shall say that there does not exist a poet (let us hope of the comic order) who from the plump bagman—none such shall be permitted to defile these aristocratic pages—seated at table with flushed face and napkin tucked under double chin, could extract not indeed a sonnet, which would be hardly fitting, but a ballad? Therefore, as every one appears to yield more or less poetry towards feeding the machines which are always at work, what further proof is needed that we are "Poets all"?

I may be a partial judge, since it is an immense advantage to a novelist—though I am not aware that the fact has been noticed—that all his *dramatis personæ* should be poets. Poets are, of course, known to be ardent wooers of the Muse; but they also love to bask generally—or to describe themselves as basking; I hope for their sakes that the half of it is true—in the smiles of beauty. Having decided that we are "Poets all," there is sure to be plenty of love-making, which, I am told, makes popular reading. It is no doubt a rather disappointing fact that so many poets are chiefly given to falling in love with themselves.

In days when the counterfeit presentments of successful men of letters are to be seen in every photographer's window cheek by jowl with the ladies of the music-hall and the professional beauties; when the lineaments of painters, famous and the reverse, are pictured by shoals in the magazines; when even their wives—if sufficiently good-looking—are hung in rows on the line in the Royal Academy; when their studios and haunts are familiar to all of us as household words, no apology is necessary for introducing my readers to a workshop fitted with machinery adapted to the manufacture of poetry.

About eleven o'clock at night two men were seated in a room in the top storey of a tall building in Pall Mall, which was let out in chambers. The apartment was æsthetically furnished, but was everywhere so littered with papers that the fashion of the almost invisible upholstery had little to do with determining its character. The chairs were hidden by heaps of books of the genus encyclopædia; on the untidy round table was a vast inkstand, and an enormous box that had once contained cigarettes; while from underneath peeped a waste-paper basket, also empty. It was the middle of January, and a fire—of as much brightness as is usually extracted from London coal —was burning on the hearth. One of the two men,

however, would have derived but little warmth from
even a more genial blaze, since his companion—if
he could be considered such—was seated with his
back to the table directly between him and the fire,
of which every flicker was thus arrested *in transitu*.
A long leg of almost impossible thinness, thrown
out on either side, formed a fire-guard, which had at
all events the effect of preventing the other tenant
of the apartment from endangering his person or
becoming oppressively warm.

The man who monopolized the fire was long and
thin, as also was his hair, which strayed in greyish
curls over the collar of his black velvet coat. He
wore a very long thin light-brown moustache, the
several hairs of which a German specialist would
have numbered in less than a lifetime. This the
long fingers of the hand not required for his cigarette
were perpetually caressing with an affection of which
it appeared to be altogether undeserving. His somewhat dissipated and anything but jovial appearance—
one feels grateful to the great majority of dissipated
people for doing their best to look jovial—was more
probably caused by the habit he had contracted of
sitting up late, smoking endless cigarettes and
drinking cold coffee, than by indulgences generally
found more captivating. A cup of the latter beverage

was even now wasting its fragrance on the mantelpiece in front of him. His countenance—if any one
could have seen it—wore an expression which would
have suggested complacent and imperturbable self-
satisfaction, had it not been slightly overshadowed
by boredom. Now and again, when he threw a
remark—as it were a bone to a dog—together with
a puff of smoke over his shoulder to the man who
was perforce sitting behind him, he presented a clear-
cut profile which, if it gave but little promise of
strength, was yet not without evidence of culture.
He had an aquiline nose and dreamy blue eyes,
which last had been trained—eyes and poodles can
be trained to anything—to wear a " far-away " look.
He had made it his business in life to look intellectual, and this business he followed with the more
success in that he was probably himself unaware
how much was affectation, and how little reality.
The impostor who can first impose on himself will
frequently have but little trouble with the rest of the
world.   The position he had taken up was suggestive
of the tone of his remarks, which, however, the man
behind him did not appear to object to.

Mr. Prothero Corthee was quite the newest, and
therefore the best poet to himself and to a few
admirers who expected to be paid in kind, and

of whom the most enthusiastic was now seated
behind him. He had an affectation of not caring
for anything that was said, even in praise of himself
—and it may be confidently asserted that to all
else his ears were hermetically sealed. Indeed, the
way in which he had now turned his back on his
guest (for Mr. Prothero Corthee was seated in his
own chambers) was a very clever piece of affectation
indeed. In fact, the new poet was distinctly clever,
and this quality was never more conspicuous—*lucus
a non lucendo*—than when he was accepting the
incense of his admirers. But it may be doubted
whether cleverness is, in the long run, of any more
advantage to a poet than to a statesman; and to
the latter it is certain, sooner or later, to prove
fatal. That the new poet was accustomed to be
anything but polite, and sometimes downright rude
to his chief admirer, was perhaps the nearest approach
he had ever made to genius.

The days are past when poets were born. They
are now made, and some of them very much made
indeed. The class of goods turned out by the general
run of modern poets—I am not speaking of the exceptions—requires a good deal of advertising. It
cannot be too often repeated that your medicine is
worth a guinea a box. But to suppose that a poet can

be advertised openly at so much a line, and in the same column perhaps as the wares of the immortal and life-giving B——, would be to be very ignorant indeed. The Muse, if slightly vulgarized, is yet a little above, if far less profitable, than chocolate or soap. Her praises must be whispered delicately, yet with the impassioned fervour of which nothing is so capable as humbug. There are occasions when the answer of the invoked Echo is inaudible.

Mr. McCawmee Jones, the other occupant of the room, was a critic, and therefore one of those who make the poets who are no longer born. The contemptuous treatment that he was receiving made him feel confident—though he should have known better—that the praises he had been for some months lavishing on his latest idol were the genuine outcome of a critical and impartial mind.

CHAPTER II.

A KINDLY CRITIC.

MR. McCAWMEE JONES presented a different exterior to that of his host. His figure, as he sat on his chair like a sack, was that of a typical John Bull run to seed. Instead of a cigarette he was puffing vehemently at an enormous cigar that he had brought with him, while on the table in front of him was a tall glass of brandy-and-seltzer—extorted with some trouble from the Poet. There was no appearance about him of refinement or ultra-sensitiveness. On the contrary, his exterior gave promise of the mental qualities to which a rhinoceros may be presumed to aspire. He had a good-natured but rather stupid face, and thick lips contracted into an almost perpetual smile. His enormous bald head was fringed with brown hair, which he wore very short indeed. He was not only a critic by profession, but a writer on every subject under the sun—and elsewhere. On

pictures, knur and spell, architecture, football, sliding-
seats, and indeed on everything, his dictum was—
by those whom he honoured with his approval—
considered law.   But it was as a critic of poetry that
he chiefly shone.   Indeed he was allowed to be *facile
princeps* among poetical critics, and if this meant that
he criticized most writers of verses, he was no doubt
entitled to the description.   There were ill-natured
people—and truth is ill-natured or nothing—who
said that previous to his full-fledged appearance as a
critic, and when addressed by his few friends as plain
" Jones," he had known but little of anything.
That he ṯhad no ear for verse or music did not
necessarily incapacitate him for criticizing either
in a day when it is a point of honour with so many
to engage in contests for which they are physically
and morally unfitted, and, the rounder they have
been fashioned by nature, to place themselves the
more determinedly in the squarer hole.

At the present moment Mr. McCawmee Jones was
a firm ally of Mr. Corthee, though any hint of
this from an outsider would have given dire offence
to the latter.   Mr. Jones, though he did not look
clever, and may not have been a very capable critic,
was no fool.   He had succeeded in thoroughly
mastering an art for which life has often been found

too short. A good deal is gained, at the commencement of a career, by deciding once for all on your *rôle*. Mr. Jones had early perceived the immense advantage possessed by a tradesman who sells absolutely indispensable wares. People are so constituted mentally and physically as to be unable to exist without two things. These two are bread and flattery. Mr. Jones had never felt any inclination to follow the calling of a baker (whose enormous and unfair profits were then in the dim and distant future), or even of a miller, and it was therefore almost of necessity that he had taken up his present calling. Whatever he might have been as a baker, as flatterer he had few equals, and with the profits of his very necessary article of commerce he had rested content, without striving to emulate the gigantic emporiums of the universal provider.

Mr. Jones had started in life without education, and was not educated now in the general acceptation of the word. But there is " a rule of thumb" in this as in other matters, and he had necessarily picked up a good deal. He was without prejudices, artistic or otherwise. Those whom he flattered believed in him—and he flattered a good many. By his persevering worship of others he had got himself to be regarded as quite a little deity. A vast number of people who wished to climb had voted him into the box to distribute passes for Parnassus. Of course there were many who thought him a quack, and would not stoop to accept his patronage. Of these independent men a considerable number—from having no sacred critic—perished, or languished unknown. Should one be successful in emerging unaided from the ruck, the critic would lose no time in taking possession of him and including himself among his admirers.

From the obscurity in which Mr. Jones's early history was involved it was impossible to proclaim with certainty that his youth had been nourished on oil. But to be able to dispense so much was surely presumptive evidence of having swallowed a good deal. It could not be truly said that he flattered everybody; he did not indeed know everybody. Those whom he did not know he either ignored altogether or damned with that faintest of praise which is the modern critic's substitute for the savage assaults of the old school.

Literary personages are never tired of reminding us that, except on rare occasions, old or even new writers need fear nothing worse—as if there could be anything worse—than to be ignored or treated with a little mild scorn, and it must be acknowledged that modern critics show an amount of tolerance which amply proves the majority to be amiable and unwilling to wound. Some may be of opinion that criticism has lost in strength what it may have gained in good-nature. The man who hesitates to crush an obnoxious insect will almost certainly be kind-hearted, but he will scarcely be of the stuff of which Bismarcks are made.

The touching advice to cast one's bread upon the waters was perhaps never literally followed, and in these days is generally neglected in its metaphorical sense. Still it has never been utterly disregarded, and in this matter-of-fact age there are people who, while declining to entrust good, sound, wholesome bread to the current, have discovered that butter has a very fair chance of returning. Though no amount of care can secure ventures of this nature from risk, the experienced outfitter is less reckless than might be imagined, and is not accustomed to make use of the best possible materials. Indeed, an inferior article makes quite as good a show, and "butterine" is a good deal cheaper than a commodity "warranted pure." Perhaps the casters of the former too often overlook the improbability of a better quality being returned to them. There are places—eddies or backwaters—where this apparently

wasteful business is so much in vogue that the waters
appear quite unpleasantly greasy.   One is reminded
how, when a boy, it was one's delight to sail a toy-
boat on a pond.   On its arrival at the opposite side
there was always a playmate ready to start it on the
return journey.

It is charitable to suppose that the habit of indiscriminately praising every one in whose company
you may find yourself, sprang originally from a
mistaken, if kindly, wish not to hurt or offend.   But
it is to be feared that it now proceeds from a morbid
desire of being praised in return.   There is, indeed,
no amount of humiliation that a toper will not put
up with rather than go without the dram which has
become a necessity.   But counterfeit praise cannot
hope to evoke a genuine return.   At the end of the
exchange both parties are exactly where they were.

It is possible for a novice, even without being very
conceited, to mistake the " butterine " for something
quite different, and to imagine that *laudari a
laudato* is necessarily a certificate of worth.   But
he will speedily be undeceived if from sincerity or
inexperience he neglects to make a quick return of
the praise with which he had been plastered.

Perhaps after all there was nothing so very
wonderful in the fact that Mr. Jones had been able

to acquire and retain a position of considerable eminence. Perseverance more often succeeds than genius, and the critic was persevering or nothing. It is possible now-a-days to obtain in a few minutes from encyclopædias and books of reference more information than would be gained in a life spent in the acquirement of any special knowledge. There might still be a few prejudiced people who, on a question, for instance, of deep sea fisheries, would prefer to utilize the experience of a practical sailor. But then prejudiced people are happily so few. To Mr. McCawmee Jones magazines—even quarterlies —opened the doors obdurately closed to so many. When he had to write an article or a review he did not go back to his experience, for he had no experience to which he could return. He did not even go out of doors. Instead he went to a book-shelf. That he made very few mistakes was partly luck, and partly cleverness and the habit of keeping his ears open—enormous ears which would have delighted Darwin. To say that he was now quite ignorant would have been to libel him as more incapable than an Irish labourer. At least he was wise in one respect, and had declined to follow the example of successful politicians and others who are fond of ostentatiously kicking down the ladder by

which they rose. He still stuck to his flattery—all
the more meritoriously on the present occasion, as
he was shut out from the fire. Fortunately for the
few, the great majority are ignorant that people
are generally taken at their own valuation, though
perhaps some of those who early grasped the value
of this great principle may have made too much use
of their advantage. Life is, indeed, like a bazaar,
where no one dreams of altering the tickets on goods
that the owners have priced too low.

Mr. Jones was speaking in his smooth, oily voice.
He had a habit of enunciating his words in a leisurely
manner, with a view, no doubt, to the producing of
as soothing an effect as possible. The Poet's interest
seemed to centre in the smoke-wreaths which his
eyes followed intently till they disappeared in the
dark corners of the room.

" By the bye "—with a sudden turn to the conversation, which had been strictly confined to the
supposed beauties of Mr. Corthee's last poem—"there
was something said about my going down with you
to Beddington next week. If you have made up
your mind I should rather like the outing, unless,
of course, you had rather go without me. I hear
it is a jolly old place, and your cousin, the Squire, is
a real good sort, and I should like to meet him again."

It was almost impossible to refrain from answering. When in Mr. Jones's company Mr. Corthee frequently kept absolute silence; and indeed the former was quite capable of carrying on a conversation unaided.

"I thought of going down there next week," he said surlily. There was a suspicion in his manner of "I am not sure I shall go now."

"I understand," Mr. Jones continued, "that your cousin, Miss Ellis, is a jolly girl"—a murmur passed the barrier of the Poet's teeth; was it possibly "damned impudence?"—"I wonder if a fellow would have any chance there?" The deprecating tone rather suggested some other fellow, but Mr. Corthee seemed highly indignant. He rose languidly, and stood with his back to the fire.

"My cousin would be sure to fall in love with you," he said, in his most bitterly sarcastic tones.

Mr. Jones winced a little, but—true to his principles—"Not if you are there," he murmured softly. The Poet carelessly accepted the homage.

"Thank you," he said superciliously, "I am not in for that sort of thing."

"I know," returned Mr. Jones. "Wedded to Muse —and all that. Glad you leave us poor devils a chance of something."

Was it possible that there was a slight tinge of
sarcasm in his tone? If so, it may be safely declared
that it passed unnoticed by the Poet, who was
passing his long fingers caressingly through his thin
hair, and who would never have dreamed of the
possibility of any one ridiculing him.

Mr. Jones rose, put on his overcoat, took his hat,
and made for the door; with his hand on the handle
he paused.

"Then shall we go?" he inquired.

"Oh, yes, we'll go," said the Poet peevishly,
looking at the door as if to add, "and I wish you'd
go now."

"Start on Tuesday, then?"

Mr. Jones waited a moment or two, but, as no
answer was vouchsafed, he opened the door and
walked out.

"What an ass that fellow is getting," he said, as
he descended the stairs. "I almost wonder I can put
up with him. He is about the worst I have had.
There isn't a redeeming feature about him. His
poems are humbug, and he is a humbug, and I am
the worst humbug of all. But how the deuce can I
help myself?"

"Bah!" snorted the Poet, when he found himself
alone, "that fellow is taking too much on himself.

What a conceited ass he is getting to be. Ha! ha!" and he laughed a discordant laugh—"a lady-killer indeed! I've a good mind to have a try myself, just to take the conceit out of him. Going down there with that snob! But one must have somebody to keep off the yokels. Hang the country, larks and things. Oh! yes, I dare say. Snow too, by Jove. Gets into your shoes, I expect. Would get a pair of boots if I had time. I won't go. Yes, I will. Hardly fair to the girl to leave her for that fellow to roll his gooseberry eyes at. She must be smart though to catch me."

So spake the Poet as he retired to rest, forgetting that a haughty spirit goes before a fall.

CHAPTER III.

BEDDINGTON, the residence of Robert Ellis, Esq., shortly to be favoured by a visit from the two literary magnates to whose symposium the reader has been introduced, was a rather fine old place in Daneshire, about seven miles from the county town of Carbury. It had but little pretension to architectural beauty, and had a rather dwarfed appearance from being surrounded by enormous trees, which had calmly outlived many generations of fretting and now forgotten humanity. The windows in the front of the house were small, and some of them had been bricked up in the days of the window-tax, and never re-opened on its repeal. The old-fashioned front door looked mean and small to modern ideas, and the flight of stone steps, guarded by a plain iron handrail, and placed at right angles to the front of the house, had at a little distance the appearance of a vast horse-block. In the centre of the roof was a cupola, under which was an old bell, which an ancestor of the present squire, who had been a noted collector of coins, had had cast from the gold and silver duplicates which he was unwilling to present to rival museums. The bell had an exquisite tone, though the present squire may have been partial in preferring it to the peals of the neighbouring churches. But he was one of those men who are to be envied in that they always consider their possessions the best in the world, and find it easy to convince themselves that what they cannot have is undesirable. In old times the bell may have had some duties above the common, but it had now to be content with the functions of a mere dinner-bell. You would not have guessed this from its tone, which was rich and full as ever. Inanimate things often set an example (in their phlegmatic way) of content under a change of circumstances, which would be well if we oftener followed.

Beddington was at present rather under a cloud; the evil days that had come upon agriculture having so reduced what had once been a fine income that the owner was forced to abstain from any outlay that did not promise to be remunerative. This got in fact to mean that he abstained as far as possible from any outlay at all. Mr. Ellis had been brought up at Eton and Oxford, but had long ago lost any taste for literature with which he may have been inoculated at either seat—so-called—of learning. The old house had been stored by a literary descendant of the numismatist, with books of which the greater part were rubbish, though amongst them were many of the old standard works which modern writers find so useful and suggestive, and an edition more or less valuable of almost every poet from Chaucer who had made any name at all—including a good many who had been unable to keep their names when they had made them. This collection it had been the accepted tradition for each succeeding squire to augment with the works of any poet who flourished in his reign. For some reason— perhaps for no more inscrutable one than that an ancestor of the present squire preferred cock-fighting to literature—there had been a pause after Byron, and the *hiatus* was now such a wide one that the then acknowledged duty of completing the collection had been deferred. The deferred task got daily—as such tasks do—more and more arduous, till gradually all hope or intention of completing it had passed by. A man who has decided to neglect an uncongenial duty soon gets to find excuses for the neglect, and thence to convince those whom it may concern that it was not a duty after all. Mr. Ellis, while knowing little of the contents of his library, had got into the habit of accounting for the abrupt cessation of the collection—which, since it was his property, could be nothing less than perfect—by saying that there were no more poets to collect. As he knew nothing at all of modern poetry, he had little difficulty in persuading himself of their non-existence; and he may also have allowed himself to imagine that ignorance of the moderns constituted him a fit champion of the ancients—of whom he knew but little more. When the generally acknowledged merits of Jones, Brown, and Robinson were brought —as occasionally happened—to his notice, the statement that they were not in his library (with the contents of which he was at least outwardly familiar) appeared to him an all-sufficient denial of their claims. There would have been no greater believer than the Squire—who was no talker—in the truth of *tout est dit*, if he had ever happened to hear of the saying. The eschewer of " conversation " has the best of things now-a-days, inasmuch as the chance of making an original remark is well-nigh hopeless, or at all events the only things that have not been said are the things that are not worth saying.

Having such negative literary tastes, and necessarily holding such a poor opinion of modern literary
men, the Squire had naturally but few acquaintances
in literary circles. But in the previous year, during
a brief stay in London, he had met at a friend's
house a young man about forty years old—at forty
a modern poet is in his first youth—whom he had
been told was the coming man. He would have
attached but little value to a pre-eminence, which
he at first likened to that of a one-eyed man among
the blind, if the new poet had not also happened to
be his cousin, though several times removed. In
ordinary circumstances he would have found considerable difficulty in accepting Mr. Prothero Corthee
as the representative of a race he had brought himself to consider extinct; but he was one of those who,
without being in the least conceited, consider that
to be in the remotest degree connected with them
is for ordinary mortals, if not a patent of nobility,
yet a sufficient certificate of merit. Without caring
at all for his new-found relative, or troubling himself
in the least about his qualifications, he soon got
into the way of talking about "my cousin the poet."
To the latter it was a pleasing, because novel, dis-
tinction to be connected with a " lord of many acres,"
whose appearance contrasted favourably with the

generality of his somewhat *blasés* associates. The news of the decadence of agriculture had not yet reached the ears of the London literary world, which indeed it would not greatly have disturbed. The Squire was on one or two occasions Mr. Corthee's guest at the literary club which he frequented, and where the visitor's old-world prejudices, which he never for a moment dreamt of concealing, proved quite a breezy sensation. The " Immortals "—the name generally used, not without pride, by members of the club, that too by which it was so generally known to the outside public as to render its more proper and legal title of little importance, if not superfluous—was the place to which hungry poets, or those whom other people thought or pretended to think poets, or the much larger number who thought themselves poets or were open to being persuaded of the fact, flocked—as others went to an eating-house—for the necessary laudatory pabulum which was denied them outside. Within its not very bright or very spacious precincts—as opium-eaters in their den—they were accustomed to compound for the neglect of cold or even contemptuous worldlings by the exchanging of mutual assurances of prospective or even actual immortality, and by agreeing to be—with some necessary classifications—poets all.

Confidence—a little too much sometimes—was rather endued than hope left behind by those who entered there.

The Squire was greatly interested if rather astonished by the strange people amongst whom he found himself, as if he were a new Gulliver. Instead of the loud and hearty tones to which he was accustomed (and which as often conveyed censure as the reverse), there were perpetually—except when the waiters were being scolded—to be heard the soft sibilant sounds of praise. Indeed, the place seemed to him a kind of church, where the religion was for the congregation to worship one another and be worshipped in turn.

The members who frequented the "Immortals" were curious-looking people of all sorts, sizes, and colours : red, black—there was a full-blooded African from Zanzibar—grey, clean-shaven, full-bearded, even occasionally dirty. All were alike in having a look of cleverness and in frequently lapsing into an attitude like that of a wild animal on the watch—this last probably when listening intently for praise. To the Squire, who had no idea or wish to pass beyond the bounds of ordinance, and who indeed expected to be buried and done with one day like the generality, it was a somewhat weird and startling experience to be brought into contact with a number of people who were secure, in their own or their friends' opinions, of immortality. He had heard, too, that the old "Immortals" on Olympus used to quarrel among themselves. Not so these modern "Immortals." All chance of any misunderstandings was removed by the banishment, or possibly only the gagging of Truth. Everybody was everything grand and good to everybody, till they passed outside the doors. It was something new to see members taking their turn as if in a barber's chair, and then rising to assist in lathering the recent operator. The spectacle would have been made perfect to a cynic—could any such have found entrance—by the fact that no one seemed conscious of any degree of absurdity. Nothing approaching to a smile, much less to jovial laughter, was ever seen on the lips of distributor or recipient of praise. The serious acceptance of hyperbolic flattery was indeed only intermitted for the equally serious return.

The Squire was no doubt laughed at behind his back—which is surely preferable to being laughed at to one's face—and on returning to his hotel he chuckled over the absurdities of his new friends. Before leaving London he had cordially, as his way was, invited the Poet and the most inseparable of his admirers to pay him a visit after Christmas, and to this visit he was now looking forward—as we are apt to contemplate self-imposed obligations thoughtlessly undertaken—with no vast amount of pleasure.

CHAPTER IV.

MAGGIE ELLIS.

THE Squire's old-fashioned hospitality was sufficient as a rule to preserve his guests from *ennui*. When he did not suffice to repel boredom, there was yet his only daughter, Maggie—he had been left a widower some years ago—in whose presence it was simply impossible for any rightly-constituted person to feel other than joyful; that is, as long as Miss Maggie did not too openly show that she preferred some one else's company. Once it was discovered by an unfortunate visitor that such was the case, the remainder of his stay, which he made as brief as possible, was an unceasing struggle with the combined forces of jealousy and weariness.

Not that Maggie was very bright, or even very beautiful. She was simply one of those fine, healthy English girls who spoil young men with any taste— the taste in such matters of the modern young man is too often conspicuous by its absence—for the clever beauties of this and other climes. She had a tall, graceful figure, which was perhaps seen to the best advantage in the saddle, where indeed it was seen very often. She had an abundance of brown hair, and bright clear eyes, whose exact colour it was not easy at a first glance to determine. Her nose was a good sensible nose, neither too long nor too short, neither Grecian nor Roman, but English— which is far better. Her lips were red (as indeed lips generally are except in novels, where they are addicted to turning white), and not too full. When they parted, as they did when she was moved to pity or joy, you got a glimpse of two rows of the whitest possible teeth. When she thought of any- thing—which was sometimes the case, though she lived in the country—she had a way of biting, or seeming to bite, her under-lip. These charms, such as they are—perhaps the last was scarcely a charm —are common to many country girls. They would not have amounted to much without her complexion. Her face was slightly embrowned by sun and air. She was not given to veils or sun-shades, and the sun returned her confidence by kissing her tenderly, never scorching or freckling her as he did so many others. As she had no pretensions to exceptional loveliness, so neither had she any claim to a great amount of cleverness or wisdom. But she had her full share of common-sense and tact, and these are more useful than the former in the affairs of every day. She was now twenty-one. Her mother had been dead three years, and since that day the management of her father's household had devolved upon her. She was not so countrified but that she had spent a portion of two seasons in London, where the admiration she excited had not been sufficient either in quantity or quality to spoil her.

With one exception, there was scarcely a thought in Maggie's breast that she would have wished to conceal, at all events from her father. The discovery that his daughter wrote poetry would have greatly astonished the Squire, and might even have had the effect of causing him to admit that there might be a poet—or a poetess, at all events—after Byron. Doubtless he would have accounted for it by remembering that the time and labour which his predecessors had given to the collecting, in the most costly bindings, of the national poetry must have made their descendant akin to the poets, and therefore not unlikely to father one. But though the Squire was unaware of the fact, Maggie had in very early days shown a predilection for putting her ideas

—or the want of them—into verse. To early
acquire the technicalities of any art is to have
smoothed the way to success. When Maggie was
about three years old she was overheard by her old
nurse—who had come upon her unseen—repeating
to herself some words which appeared to give her
infinite happiness. The old woman listened carefully, in the expectation, from the rapt expression of
the child's face, that she would hear something sweet
and rare as angels' whispers. She was disappointed
to find that the words were apparently mere doggerel,
though to the child they may have contained some
deep or pathetic meaning. It was clear, however,
that even at that early age Miss Margaret Ellis had
an ear for rhyme, for which some modern poets
would give the appendages they are unconscious of
wanting. And this was what the nurse overheard—

> " Curl-paper, curl-paper ;
> Widdledy, widdledy, whirl-paper."

If in the case of these probably impromptu rhymes
there was but little sense behind the words, there
have no doubt been instances of poets long past any
but their second childhood who have divorced reason
from rhyme quite as absolutely. Even when Maggie
had improved on her first attempts by the addition
of sense and feeling, she kept her secret closely

hidden in her own bosom. This not from any fear of running counter to her father's prejudice—which she must have known she could easily d.s.ipate—but from a feeling that to talk about emotions which seemed to her almost as sacred as prayer, would be to vulgarize if not to destroy them. It was strange, perhaps, that she should have had this feeling in these days when *scribimus indocti doctique poemata*, and when scarcely any one dreams of affecting exemption from a disease which, equally with measles, appears to be the common lot of modern humanity. A further reason for hiding her talent was that she thought it a very small one, and had not the conceit necessary for a competition with larger capitalists. Though she was only a country girl, and not particularly accomplished at that, she had learnt—as children sometimes run before they walk—the rare lesson of self-knowledge about as well—which is not saying much—as it is generally known. She was aware that she was good-looking, nor did she need to be told—though people were always telling her—that she rode well. For the latter accomplishment perhaps some praise might be due to her; but her poems—which after all were not many—were like the lark's song, which it may be guessed he cannot help uttering. The spontaneous

D

outcome of a charming combination of health, happiness, and fine weather must be pleasing, but was not of necessity meritorious. Human beings are exceptional in often wishing to conceal some fardel which nature has ordained they shall carry; and indeed it is well to remember that these, whether good or bad—like a beautiful woman's face, or the excrescence of a hunchback—are not ours by merit or ill-deserving. Maggie's rhymes were not always faultless, nor were her metres—for which she went to her father's library—anything very wonderful. There was much the same difference between her artless productions and the performances of the professional poet that there is between the self-binding reaping-machine, with its elaborate and noisy arrangements for shearing the stubble, and the almost extinct reaper with his "broad hook," whose careful sheaves were tied one by one by the wife—sun-kissed, like Hood's Ruth—who followed in his wake. Her baby nestled under a carefully-arranged shelter of sheaves hard by, and thither she repaired once and again to admire—she was never tired of admiring—the sleeping beauty. The "self-binder" gets through an enormous amount of work, and does it, I am told, cheaply; so the woman can stay at home—the best place for her, of course. The man—he never imagined a day would come when he would cease to be proud of his art—may hang up his "broad hook," and look moodily over the garden gate at the big machine whirling off its unlimited supply of sheaves.

Maggie's poems were on subjects with which she was familiar, and which therefore she did not have to "read up." They were evoked by a chance remark, or by some scene in the landscape as she rode with her father. She would never have dreamt of writing on what she did not feel, or except when words were, so to speak, forced out of her. She scarcely imagined that there were people so clever, or so silly, as to turn out poems as tailors do clothes, "to order," and with as much feeling—it must be allowed, too, with as much precision—as a machine.

Of love she had never written a line, and indeed she knew little about it. Had she known more she would have kept the knowledge to herself. Doubtless, had she flattered herself that she was a poetess, she would have taken credit for insight into this as into other matters.

CHAPTER V.

THE COMING GUESTS.

MAGGIE and her father lived a great deal alone. The distance at which the Hall was situated from a railway-station prevented fashionable, or pseudo-fashionable, people from journeying into what they were pleased to call "the wilds." The few, how-ever, who ventured were received with a hearty welcome now-a-days seldom met with, and were tempted, when the opportunity offered, to venture again. In the shooting season a few neighbours would be asked to shoot, but the shooting was not very good. It was beginning to be recognized—rather late in the day—that the preservation of farmers is after all of more importance than that of fur or feather.

At other times the Squire was accustomed to spend a good portion of each morning with his bailiff, studying ways and means. He had years ago given up his hunting, as he thought that he could no longer afford it, or at all events that, as his tenants could no longer afford it, it was his duty to follow suit. His doing so was no doubt a mistake. A man in the Squire's position cannot afford to retire from communication with his neighbours, and this was nowhere better kept up than in the hunting-field. It is true that some of these neighbours had given the same reason for their withdrawal. Even the tradesmen from Carbury, a few of the wealthiest of whom had in days past hunted occasionally, now ceased to do so, either because they thought it bad taste to indulge in a sport from which the owners of the land were debarred, or because—dependent, as most of them were, on agriculture—they too felt the pressure of the bad times.

In fact, the chief patrons now of the Clayland Hunt—and they were not very paying ones—were strangers who patronized the district because it was less crowded and cheaper than the Shires. They also found that it was possible to give themselves airs among these yokels—as they called them—on which they would not have ventured elsewhere. The Squire felt by no means inclined—though he was neither very proud nor very sensitive—to ride

over his own fields in company with or perhaps in
the rear of strangers who were certain to be better
mounted, and would very likely go better than the
owner of the soil. Yet, after all, if he had been
as keen as he once was, he would scarcely have
allowed the fear of being outridden on his own land
to deprive him of what had been his favourite sport.
He may have been conscious that he was growing
old, and if so, it would be soothing to find an excuse
for his abstinence less humiliating than a failure of
nerve. He still spent a good deal of his time on
horseback. For hours every day, regardless of
weather, he would be riding over the estate on his
sturdy cob, and few landowners knew their farms
and their tenantry better than he did. Some of his
tenants indeed considered that he knew too much,
and would have exchanged him not unwillingly for
one whose ways might have been less pleasant and
whose word less to be depended on, but whom it
might have been possible occasionally to hoodwink.
Sometimes Maggie accompanied her father in his
morning rides: more generally she was occupied
with household affairs. After lunch the Squire and
his daughter were inseparable. Very friendly relations were still kept up with a few old families
similarly circumstanced, while the *nouveaux riches*

who had recently become squires by purchase—and wished they had not—were as far as possible ignored. It may have struck the Squire that Maggie would one day be leaving him, but he did not consider it his duty to hasten her departure; while the possibility that the temptation to quit might come from one of the new county families certainly never entered his head. Maggie was, to all appearance, fancy free. There were no curates in the neighbourhood who could be considered at all eligible; the old parson who had held the living for twenty years, and was likely to hold it for about as many more, had no son, and it had never struck him that his duty to his old friend demanded of him the engagement at great inconvenience to himself of a useless but "suitable" young man.

The Rev. Allen Butler, formerly Fellow of New College, Oxford, had greatly astonished all his friends and admirers by accepting the living of Beddington when it had been decided that Oxford was the sphere in which he was calculated to shine. He and the Squire had been undergraduates together, and his old friend was probably the only person who was aware of his reasons for rusticating. These reasons some had connected with religious scruples, while others had suspected that it was a disappointment in love which had turned the whole current of his life. Whatever the cause, his career, with all its possibilities, came to an abrupt ending. He had stopped —like the Squire's library—at a certain point, and the gap between him and modern thought was now too wide to be bridged over. His interest in literature ceased, when he left Oxford, to be progressive, and he was blind to any progress with which he had not kept pace. As the Squire's library was the only one to which he had access, he soon ceased to notice its deficiencies. At first he no doubt grumbled a little at its antiquity, but the Squire's " Nonsense, man ; it's not worth getting, I tell you," when he wanted a book which was even comparatively modern, had the effect, if not of satisfying, of silencing him. Gradually he became the recognized champion of a view which the Squire had only accepted to save himself from " bother." He was so far right that the longest life is too short for the study of half the books well worth study which were written generations before we were born. To fly from these to the modern is to neglect what is certainly good for what may very possibly be skin-deep and superficial.

There came a day when the parson, while affecting more ignorance than he had of modern literature,

had got to be a little more conceited than he had a
right to be on account of knowledge, which after all
was not very thorough. It was certainly natural
and perhaps even wise to believe that the arena
from which he had retired had no longer any prizes
to attract, and it may have made him less unhappy
in his obscurity to feel sure that those left behind to
carry on the contest had degenerated. I must confess that the Rector's sole claim to be admitted a
member of the firm of " Poets all " was that in his
college days he had shone as a writer of Latin verse.
But it is absurd to be too scrupulous in a question
affecting one's own particular hobby-horse. Some
years after coming down to Beddington he had
married a middle-aged spinster connected with a
county family, who, on the death of Maggie's mother,
and assisted by the Squire's purse, had willingly
entered upon the vacant position of Lady Bountiful.
For the rest he felt towards the Squire as a brother,
and towards Maggie more as a second father even
than an uncle. He was a noble-looking man, with a
head which would have looked well, as was once the
general anticipation, under a mitre. He had left
Oxford before Donnishness had become quite a
second nature—a Don too late transplanted to the
country is a fearful thing—and the scrupulousness

with which he performed duties to which he might easily have imagined himself superior, had, assisted by his air and appearance, made him friends of the whole parish. Notwithstanding Mr. Butler's disinclination to provide the curate, whom so many in the country have learnt to consider a cheap and almost indispensable luxury, neither the Squire— whom the advent of a youthful ecclesiastic would perhaps not have greatly cheered—nor his daughter were conscious of feeling in the least dull. They may have been so, but as they never knew it, ignorance, as in many previous cases, was bliss. Both were apparently contented with a simple round of duties—the poor were always with them—alternating with what most people would scarcely have considered pleasures. Happiness should accompany the power of making others happy, and one need not wander far in the country to find those who are worse off than one's self. Unfortunately the fact that the search is so easy causes it to be too frequently neglected.

On the evening of the day preceding that on which the visitors were to arrive the Squire and Maggie were engaged in the drawing-room after dinner in talking them over. To Maggie the expected guests were unknown, and on that account she had invested them with the qualities in which some of her intimates were deficient. Maggie was too human not to feel some pleasurable excitement about those whom she had decided would be very dissimilar and perhaps—she allowed it was possible— very superior to the old. While always the reverse of discontented, she was not unconscious of an un- satisfied craving for friendship—or was it for love ?— other than she had known. She had sometimes wished that, like a bird, she could soar above her surroundings. But to soar she must have wings. Given wings, a teacher would be required to show her how to use them. Her mother, had she lived, might have been her instructress—here Maggie was probably in error—but her father thought that his level was high enough for all mortal desires. She was not unaware of the power exercised by women under circumstances in which she was unlikely to be placed. Maggie had had her little triumphs, which she had neither sought very eagerly nor greatly valued when won, and she was desirous—what girl would not be ?—of trying new pastures. She would like—but what did she know about it ?—to conquer on some field where victory was a little less a matter of course, and a little more glorious than she had found it. To a maiden every new male friend is a possible knight-errant and deliverer from what she may scarcely have acknowledged a prison.

" To-morrow," said the Squire, with humorous ruth, " we shall be no longer alone. We shall have to mind our p's and q's. I've been letting myself grow rusty."

" Oh, papa ! you haven't, I'm sure."

" I shall be pleased for you to see some one more modern, my dear. This Poet, our cousin, is a wonder, I've been told, though I am quite unable to credit it. You must learn him. It is too late for me to learn new poets, if there are any, which I don't believe. Even if there were, as some silly person has been writing, fifty-two (or even fifty-three) new poets, I would have nothing to do with them. The old ones are as much as I can manage. It is odd that some of these new planets have not swum into our ken. But then there might be a new planet every night without my being much the wiser. I wouldn't get out of my bed for the biggest they are likely to find. You are different, of course. Your cousin's friend the Critic is also, by all accounts, a wonderful man, but not much to look at ; of the two I like him the better. You will probably prefer the Poet—as he calls himself. I wonder if they are fond of country life. If not, we can show them little else. Nor is it likely that anything else would please them, as everything but the country is better in town. Any poet but a sham one should revel in country life, not that he should always live there, but it is the country from which he should get his ideas. The ideas drawn from a street, curbed and guttered, would not be very grand—unless, of course, there happened to be a bonnet shop over the way. We will go to the meet at Apley Wood the' day after to-morrow. A good shaking up will do them both good—poor devils !—and they cannot come to much harm. We can just manage to mount them both. I will ride my cob, and you will take your pony. On the next day we will shoot. There is a stray pheasant or two left. Of course our friends cannot get much shooting in London, where the people are a good deal too thick on the ground, and they are probably not first-rate shots. Perhaps it will be safer to omit that part of the programme. I have already, as you know, three No. 5 shot in the left side of my head. Both these people are certain to be very polite to you. These town folk are for ever bowing and scraping. They will flatter you—or they would if it were possible. They are not likely to have seen many girls like my Maggie. Mind that little head doesn't get turned."

" Oh, papa! don't, please, talk such nonsense."

" It is not nonsense, my dear. However, I don't want to talk it."

And the Squire took his candle and departed.

CHAPTER VI.

VARIOUS reasons had combined in inducing Poet
and Critic to accept the invitation to Beddington.
Both were moved by the almost certainty of homage
a little more genuine than that to which they were
accustomed. Both, too, may have been more than
a little weary of the inevitable, and too often un-
profitable, return which might on this occasion be
omitted. The Poet had also a praiseworthy desire
to see the country. So might a merchant wish to
visit the territory the sale of whose produce had
enriched him. He had been a denizen of the great
city for many years, and his brief holidays had either
been spent abroad or in places where the country
had been made as far as possible to resemble town.
He had not, however, escaped the necessity—common
to all poets, good, bad, or indifferent—of attempting

the portrayal of rural joys, and he had discovered, to
his subsequent annoyance, that nothing is easier
than to make idiotic mistakes in describing what
you have not seen. He was uneasily conscious of
having come a "cropper" or two, and was anxious
to avoid another fall which might be as serious and
have as lasting effect as Lucifer's. To his intense
disgust, and that of about three-score more of hard-
working and ambitious "minor" poets, whose avoca-
tions and sympathies confined them to town, the
country, after having long been—from the sonneteer's
and ballad-writer's point of view—under a cloud,
was fast coming into fashion again. One reason for
this may have been that it had lost its former vulgar
air of well-fed prosperity, which was even then rather
deceptive, and was developing instead a pathetic
appearance of unkempt and half-starved poverty
which appealed to the sympathies of the money-
making crowd, and demanded to be "treated"
poetically. It had been hard—if not impossible—
to work oneself up into raptures about a lot of jovial
farmers with faces shining from the over-plenty of a
" farmer's ordinary."

High-falutin' descriptions of the country drawn
from old-fashioned writers (who had never known
more about their subject than poor Shenstone when

he wrote his " pastorals "), or evolved from one's own
ideas had been considerably overdone, and could
never have delighted any one who was not equally
ignorant. The world was getting smaller and better
known every day, and the town was making longer
incursions into the country. The ignorance which
used to write of country-folk as if they were stage
shepherds and shepherdesses was no longer excusable
or—which mattered a good deal more—saleable.

It is very sad that we moderns should have lost
the gift of knowing everything by intuition, but the
fact has to be faced, and unfortunately the gift was
never more needed than now. The Poet recognized
unwillingly that it was his duty to posterity to lose
no time in studying larks—and things—if he intended to continue writing about them. He had
also been piqued by the Critic's rude mention of the
" jolly girl." Not only was he conscious of a jealous
feeling which would not permit of his friend " walking over," but it struck him all at once that an
experience of girls, whether " jolly " or not, was as
necessary to a poet who aimed at being perfect as a
knowledge of country life. Of the word " jolly " he
had little comprehension, and he knew nothing of
girls. Of women—very artificial ones mostly, and
the more artificial they were the better he liked

E

them—he had not been without some rather trying
experiences; but he could not remember ever to
have come across a genuine unaffected girl, such as
he supposed that his unknown cousin must be.
What opportunities, indeed, had the poor creature
ever had for being anything else? Let it not be
supposed for one moment that our Poet's modesty had
restrained him from writing about the class of idyllic
woman whom yet he had never seen. Indeed, he
had written about them a good deal; and as the
background of these fancy portraits was invariably
filled in with descriptions of the country which he
did not know, prejudiced folk who knew nice country
girls laughed them to scorn. Perhaps their ridicule
mattered little, since the opinions of the very few
country people who read any new poetry scarcely
ever penetrated into the laudatory circle of the
Poet's admirers, and had no effect when they
arrived. Poets and painters, and novelists too, may
be right in sticking to their monstrosities, which may
be easier of production than more simple and, to the
generality, more pleasing representations. Of all
virtues which poets should possess, the knowledge
of a true woman is the least easy to assume. The
Poet decided to go down into the country and
make a study of a country girl. Perhaps he hardly

realized that his calling might have entailed a more disagreeable duty.

The Critic's reasons were not far to seek. He really wanted a change. His unctuous tones had become a weariness to him, and he hoped that in the country it might be permitted him to unbend so far as perhaps to swear at some one or something. He felt like a country mayor suffocating in official dress, and longing to don once more the shooting-jacket from which he has been lately debarred. He was sick of the perpetual flattery which was demanded of him, and something within was always whispering that he might be capable of better things, or at least of something less sickening. When a man begins to acknowledge himself a sham, there is a hope that he is beginning to be real. He was going to Beddington as to a place where he would be able to speak his mind—if he still had one; to be clean for a time even should he have to return to his wallowing, and that he would have to return he sadly feared. He knew too well the difficulty of permanently ousting what had become a second nature. He might expel it temporarily by a visit to the country, as with a pitchfork, but it had acquired—like everything in England—vested interests. Indeed, his second reason showed clearly

that he did not desire a permanent change. He had
lately been invited to contribute, to a magazine of
some standing, a series of articles on country sports.
To enable him to do so it was absolutely necessary
that he should see such of these as were carried on
in the winter season, and that of the others he
should obtain some particulars at second-hand. No
doubt something in the country air would come to
his aid. He felt too modest to write of recondite
affairs of which even the names were unfamiliar.

The two friends had arranged to start from London
so as to arrive at Beddington a little before dinner-
time. The afternoon was chilly, and, notwithstanding his wraps, the Poet soon began to wish himself
back at his club. He showed the most intense, if
unreasoning, disgust at finding that quite a number
of very ordinary-looking people had also chosen this
day for travelling. A poet, he thought, should be
a being apart. Where could all these red-faced
people—who might have been hop-pickers for aught
he knew or cared—with their little baskets of fish
be going to? If it had depended on him he felt
that their journey and destination would be, to say
the least, disagreeable. But he could not interest
himself in the pushings and gaspings of such a
vulgar horde. As he stood on the platform in

scornful contemplation, a fat bagman nearly swept
him off his legs with a large sharp-edged tin box,
and a brusque, "Where on hearth are you coming
to?" "Sir," the bruised Poet commenced—but the
enemy was already fifty yards away. There should
be a law, he imperiously decided, to regulate traffic
and keep nine-tenths of the vulgar fellows—who
could not really have any good reason for travelling
—at home. It is to be feared that the Poet resembled
Lady Godiva in objecting to be looked at, while he
yet laid himself out by costume and bearing to
attract observation. I have often asked myself in
vain why fantastic habiliments should be deemed
necessary auxiliaries to a poetical reputation : why
the "Muse" can only be courted as long as the
barber, poor man, is avoided. That the last is a
person to be, as far as may be, shunned I readily
allow, but why by poets more than by other people?
A whisper comes to me that quacks are notorious
for striving to catch the eyes of their dupes-to-be
with outlandish apparel, and that only sham poets
would stoop to such paltry affectations. But then
this would be very hard on Mr. Prothero Corthee.
Let a true poet wear what he likes, or nothing at
all ; we can but be grateful for his appearance.

Unlike his companion, the farther the Critic got

from town the better he began to feel. He would actually have opened the window had not the Poet shivered at the idea. They had provided themselves with a selection of papers, chiefly literary, which would have served the Squire for a year's reading, and wherein were some laudatory notices on the most recent effusions of Mr. Corthee. On alighting at the station, the Squire's comfortable old-fashioned carriage awaited them. The young country footman opened his mouth wide with astonishment at the sight of the two guests. On the Poet's head was a broad-brimmed, white billy-cock, which he had pulled over his eyes, and from under which his thin greyish locks floated out behind. He wore a Tennysonian-looking mantle, whose enormous capes enfolded him after the fashion of an antiquated jarvey. The feeble station-lamps had yet little difficulty in illuminating the fat legs of the Critic, the lower portion of which had been encased, for their visit to the country, in bright red knickerbockers with black stripes. The Poet, without troubling himself about such sublunary affairs as luggage, proceeded at once to the carriage, in which he lay back with closed eyes while Mr. Jones superintended the removal of the joint effects. The soothing tones in which the latter pointed out the various properties were a

revelation to the footman, whose first words on
climbing to his seat beside the coachman were,
" My, Bill, ain't the cove an oily one ! "

The road, without passing through the town, dived
at once into the country.   The night was star-lit,
but only mist and the steam that rose from the
horses could be seen in the light of the lamps on
either side.   The lodge was reached at last, and the
carriage swept rapidly up the long winding drive.
The Hall door was open, and a bright light shone
out from the interior into the darkness.   The two
travellers disembarked and mounted the steps, at
the top of which they were received by their host.
After being disencumbered of wraps, the Squire
ushered them into the drawing-room, where his
daughter awaited them not without eagerness.

CHAPTER VII.

THE NEW "STUDY."

I SCARCELY dare to hint at a doubt of the truth of any of those universally-accepted proverbs which so many consider, like old wine, improve with age, and which generations ago, when the wisdom of many was put into compendious form by the wit of one, may have had presumptive evidence in their favour. But if, as has been wisely said, even " Religions wear out in some thousand years without a slight refreshment from the spheres," it is hard to see why immortality should be predicated for proverbs. No doubt some proverbs—however delusive and untruthful—incite meritoriously to good works, and these I should wish to retain, since the believer, when disappointed of his expected reward, may reap other if less tangible advantages.

Perhaps one of the most delusive of proverbs is that which tells you that, " It is better to be born

lucky than rich." So few people know what to do
with their luck when they get it, and Luck—like a
scorned beauty—is so exceedingly touchy, that I
think if I had the choice, and could make a new
start, I should prefer being brought into the world a
baby millionaire to being born lucky. To the man
who had once been rich—however unlucky—some
remains of his gold almost always adhere, and, even
to the pauper who appears to have lost all, the
prestige of ruin is a little mine. Indeed, it is almost
impossible for the most reckless spendthrift to
divest himself of every rag and appear financially
naked before the world.

But Luck! She stoops over you, let us say, and
kisses you while you are sleeping, and may be gone
before you knew you had a visitor; or perhaps, if
you wake, you don't know what to do with her. As
I said, she is so touchy. My experience is that once
she is gone it is a hard matter to whistle her back.
I confess I don't care to argue about those cases in
which—like Fortunatus's purse—there is always
another slice of luck forthcoming for the man who
has thrown away his first. If any such cases could
be imagined, it is certain that nothing could be more
demoralizing.

Now the Poet had undertaken the journey—

Doctor-Syntax-like—in search of a "study," and, if he had only known it, he was now to be presented with an invaluable one. How was he going to utilize his stroke of luck? If but some friend had been at his elbow to prompt him as to his behaviour! Maggie was actually willing to take him at his own valuation. If it was generally known how many people are ready to take us at the price at which we ticket ourselves, it is to be feared there would be an awful crop—it is big enough already in all conscience—of impostors.

The room in which the travellers found themselves was old-fashioned, though by the bright fire-light it looked cosy and cheerful enough. Its great length was lighted in the daytime by three small and narrow windows, the large window which the architect had designed for the end of the room having been bricked up in the days of the window-tax, and never re-opened. There are people who imagine that this much-abused tax took its rise less from the needs of the Exchequer (now flourishing from the imposition of a duty on "thirsty" casks) than from a wise objection felt by our ancestors— or more probably ancestresses—to parading themselves, under all circumstances, in cross-lights. Now-a-days, when the race is (if the old counterfeit

presentments may be trusted), to put it mildly, no
lovelier than formerly, the usual arrangement of the
architect-builder is to throw light on your careworn
modern-business-man's countenance from every side.
Not a corner does this self-sufficient tradesman leave
you into which to retire with a reasonable hope of
rendering your ill-temper or ugliness, or both, a little
less conspicuous. His plan might be all very well
in a church where the cross-lights which find you
out are, if humiliating, no doubt improving, and
where even the unconscious display of vulgarity or
ill-breeding may have a salutary effect on the
beholders. The dwellers in private houses erected
in or which had their windows blocked up in the
days of the window-tax have—as also in some few
other matters—the best of it. It may be partly
owing to this long-abandoned restriction that the
tempers and manners of the descendants of the old
families are apparently so superior to those of the
nouveaux riches, who have been placed by the
erectors of their new dwellings, as it were, in glass
houses, through the windows of which every un-
amiable contortion and every wrinkle is evident to
the most careless observer.

If the furniture of the drawing-room was—as
must be granted—old-fashioned, there was no doubt

as to its being a woman's room. Everywhere, on every table, in every corner, there was evidence of female occupation. It seemed strange, when you had time to think about it, that the occasional presence of one woman could dominate so large a space. There were plenty of books lying about, but these were evidently not out of the Squire's library, who indeed effaced himself as far as possible when he entered the drawing-room. The room was rendered almost a sacred place to him from the fact that the wife he had long lost, and whom he still lamented, had lived a great part of her life in it. He would not willingly have allowed a table or chair to be removed, and his daughter was at least as well satisfied as her father with what had so long sufficed her mother.

Maggie came forward with a charming blush and greeted the new arrivals. For the moment she took no notice of any one but the Poet. She had never knowingly touched the hand of a poet before, and no doubt expected to feel a sort of electric thrill. In this she was disappointed, as the hand that the Poet protruded, on a level with his chin, was of a fish-like temperature, and imparted nothing but a chill. As she tremblingly encountered the glance which he turned on her—with a view to the immediate com-

mencement of his "study"—she blushed again.
"This wonderful being," she was thinking : "he is
looking into my soul." Had the glance been as
introspective as it was in reality inoperative, there
would , yet have been little cause for the blushes
which could scarcely make her look more charming.
Had she had a glass in her bosom no thought
would have been discovered a sight of which would
not have made an ordinary—or even an extraordinary
—mortal purer and better. After a word or two,
the uttering of which she was surprised, if a little
relieved, to find would not have over-taxed the
intelligence of the most commonplace being, the
Poet sauntered away from her, and proceeded to
seat himself in the most comfortable chair which
commanded a view of her face.

Maggie wondered, but had now to greet Mr. Jones,
whom she inwardly hoped would more nearly
resemble the beings she was accustomed to. At a
first glance she easily discovered that there was
nothing very terrible in his appearance. He commenced with his usual dropping fire of meaningless
nothings. Maggie's perplexed but half-amused look
startled him into remembering that he was in a strange
country not yet opened up to trade. One day no
doubt flattery would be a very necessary commodity

here, as elsewhere. He hastily concluded his sweet
phrases, and waited for the reply which experience
had taught him might be expected even from those of
less than ordinary vanity. But Maggie said nothing.

Gradually the air of surprise with which she had
listened to him gave way to a look of amusement.
Her eye roved quickly from the top of his large bald
head down to the red stripes on his knickerbockers.
Nature had clearly not intended him for a flatterer.
Mr. Jones was not insensible to the change; but,
instead of feeling aggrieved, it was as if a weight
had suddenly dropped from his shoulders. There was
something enjoyable in the new sensation of being
laughed at to one's face. His rather red features got
still redder. Gradually the lips which had adapted
themselves, as their manner was, to the administra-
tion of soft-sawder formed themselves into quite a
genuine smile. Then he broke into a little natural
laugh. Suddenly he began talking quite unaffectedly.
The return to a natural manner was as interesting
as the learning of a new art. Maggie was relieved,
when her astonishment at the transformation had
a little diminished, to find that her guests were not
both prodigies. The Critic even bore some resemblance
to the beings she was accustomed to. She glanced
towards the Poet as if to ask pardon for preferring

the commonplace, and then turned again to Mr. Jones. It was strange how sensible the latter could be when he retired, as it were, from business, or gave up the affectations which he was accustomed to regard as his stock-in-trade.

The Squire and Maggie encountered for a few moments before dinner. Said the Squire, "Dear me! What could we have been thinking of? We have never bought Cousin Corthee's book. What shall we do? Even if he isn't a poet—and I don't believe he is—he is a relation, you know. Goodness! child, we shall have to talk poetry. Can you help? *Broken Heart-strings*, wasn't that the name of his last? Broken fiddlesticks' ends! These new people don't care a straw about the old writers—their fathers, so to speak. The present generation is sadly irreverent, or I could soon settle them. They sneer at Byron, and all of them; Shakespeare too, for aught I know; and everybody I have got in my library. Tell you what, Maggie; we'll have a competition : Ancient and Modern. Not hymns exactly. Let's see. To-morrow we hunt; have the parson up in the evening. They'll find the parson a hard nut to crack. 'Twill keep me awake after hunting" —a rash asseveration. "We'll see what these moderns are made of. Hush! here they are."

On the summons to dinner the Poet came forward
as Maggie's escort. They led the way into the
dining-room, followed by the Squire and Mr. Jones.
The Squire, who felt himself in capital form, began
with a praiseworthy attempt to enliven matters,
but the game that he started in hopes of providing
sport for his guests went away without being shot
at. Hunting, shooting, even the question of "rates,"
which the Squire had fancied of universal interest,
failed to arouse any discussion. What on earth, he
thought, had these people come down to the country
for ? Mr. Jones took refuge in his unctuous smile of
unwearying solicitude, and the Poet trifled with an
excellent dinner in a way which his host felt almost
as an insult. The latter began to feel indignant and
then disgusted. Maggie fell to wondering whether
three great minds—she had scarcely a doubt, as yet,
of their greatness—were very desirable. Mr. Jones,
who made several unsuccessful attempts at being
natural again, flustered her by the absurd way in
which he laid his remarks, as it were, at her feet.
Fortunately the Poet's seeming neglect, to which
she was as little accustomed, tended to keep her
cool. She was beginning to be aware that her high
expectations of enjoyment were in danger of being
disappointed—unless, indeed, she might by and by

have the courage to laugh. But as yet it was uncertain whether there would even be anything to laugh at.

When Maggie left the table the Squire hoped for an improvement. He passed the decanters with a gaiety he was far from feeling, and started once more on politics. But the Poet, who had lit a cigarette, gave a perceptible shudder.

"We care nothing for these things," the Critic hastened to remark; the suggestion being that they were beneath the notice of intellectual people. The Squire, who had some sense of humour, began to be more amused than angry. Possibly he acknowledged that there was a glimmer of sense in keeping out of politics.

"If they won't have politics," he said to himself, "they must wait a bit for poetry. I don't feel up to it all alone. To-morrow they shall have it hot from the parson."

An adjournment was presently made to the billiard-room. But the visitors—after the Poet had succeeded in cutting the cloth—began to yawn, and the Squire encouraged their wish for an early retiring. "Remember," he said before parting, "that we hunt to-morrow."

"Delightful," said the Critic—who would have

been just as enthusiastic if his host had reminded him that he was to be hanged—as if he were in the habit of catching a fox or two every morning. He was, in truth, rather frightened, but supposed it would be all right, as he had managed to get through with other things of which he had started in equal ignorance. The Poet said nothing. Possibly he had not heard. He did not look like one to whom the joys of the chase were likely to prove enthralling. .

"I hope it will be all right," thought the Squire, "but it is a little risky. I don't like to see fellows funk, but there are, no doubt, occasions when discretion is the better part of valour. I fancy this may be one of them."

CHAPTER VIII.

THE PURSUIT OF "COPY."

THE next morning opened brightly. There had been a slight frost in the night, but not sufficient to stop hunting, and when the two Londoners came down to breakfast the sun was shining in at the windows. The Squire, in his top-boots and black coat—he had discarded "pink"—was engaged in opening his letters. Maggie, behind the urn, was looking more charming than ever in her well-fitting habit. Each of the late-comers as he addressed her let his eyes rest for a moment longer than was absolutely necessary on her face. Consciousness of the reason for such prolonged criticism may have caused her to overlook its rudeness. As it was, a slight blush reddened still more the rosy cheek. The Squire looked up from his letters with a cheery "Good-morning," but this salutation he soon supplemented with a note of astonishment.

"Hulloa!" he exclaimed. "Aren't you going to hunt to-day?"

Mr. Jones looked up from his plate.

"Why, certainly," he answered, with his mouth full; "I understood so."

The Squire started on a journey to the sideboard ostensibly in search of cold meats, but in reality to inspect the Poet's nether garments.

"Not in those clothes, I should think," he said, casting a rather disgusted glance at the latter where he sat silent and self-absorbed. "Those thin trousers of yours, Corthee, won't do at all. Simply, man, you'd be half dead by the time you got back," and the Squire laughed. "We'll see what we can do for you after breakfast."

The Poet looked, as he doubtless felt, annoyed at such slighting mention—and in Maggie's presence too—of what he had considered characteristic and appropriate attire. But he had the sense to see the truth of it. Maggie fortunately appeared to be paying no attention.

"I do not mean to hunt to-day, thank you," he said brusquely, and as if the refraining was an exception. "I should like to see the hunt, though, if the dogs' meet is not too far off. Not that I am going to train for a sporting novelist."

"You might train for something worse," said the Squire, with a laugh. "Oh yes, we'll have you driven to the 'dogs' meet,'" he added, with a feeling of relief that he would not have to show himself at the covert side with such an unsportsmanlike-looking fellow. "Now," he went on, turning towards Mr. Jones, "what can we do with you? Excuse my saying so, but those striped affairs won't do at all. I can rig you out, I dare say; we are about of a height. What would you like to have? There's my old pink will just suit you. I never wear it now. And you must try for once to get into a pair of my breeches and tops. Then you'll look quite spicy," he ran on good-naturedly, "and astonish our friends at the club when you relate your experiences."

Mr. Jones smiled nervously. He thought it very likely that his appearance in the costume mentioned would astonish more than the people at the club— who after all would not see him.

"What say you, then?" said the Squire. "If you've finished breakfast, my man will see to you at once. We've no time to lose."

Mr. Jones had finished breakfast—rather abruptly indeed, for he felt a sudden loss of appetite—and would have liked a little more time in which to make up his mind. True, he had come down to see

the country, and the best way to see the country was
to do—or try to do—as the natives did, provided
always that the attempt did not involve a broken
neck. Experience—in this world at least—accompanied with a broken neck would not be particularly
valuable, and it would be preferable to go on, as he
had managed to do for some time, without either.
He could write his sporting articles out of an encyclopædia. Suddenly the thought struck him that the
Poet was going to drive—or be driven—humbly, in a
pony-carriage. He might never have a better opportunity of eclipsing him. He would take his own
line, as fox-hunters called it. Some knowledge of
equitation might even arrive to him with the
Squire's breeches. Miss Ellis—Maggie should see
that he could risk his precious limbs in order to be
near her. Besides, after all, a day's hunting did not
mean "sudden death"—which name, he had heard,
Oxford men bestowed on buttered crumpets. The
immortal words of the great Jorrocks came into
his head with a reassuring effect: "The image of
war without its guilt, and only five-and-twenty per
cent. of its dangers." Surely he was not going to be
scared by the five-and-twenty per cent. If only the
horse would not jump about! But he supposed they
always jumped about. If only he might sit behind

the saddle! But the Squire was waiting for his answer. "Here goes," thought Mr. Jones, "'Faint heart never won fair lady.' By Jove, she is fair. If risking my neck would win her, she is as good as won already." Then aloud, "If the horse is very quiet, I shall be delighted to accept your offer of a rig-out."

The Squire looked pleased. He foresaw no danger to his guest, whom he hastened to assure that the quadruped to which he was to be entrusted was a very sober animal indeed. He lost no time in putting Mr. Jones into "his man's" hands, and in a quarter of an hour the Critic reappeared in full hunting costume. Whether the science of equitation had come to him with the Squire's clothes it was impossible for him to say, but he felt far less nervous than when he had left the room, and would probably have assented to the doctrine that there are occasions when the tailor makes the man.

Secretly he had been congratulating himself that though he had never before been on horseback, he was not quite such a novice as he might have been. There are occasions when a man who has risen can look back with gratitude to his experiences. Mr. Jones—though nobody in his little world appeared to be aware of the fact, or would have thought any the worse of him for what was not even his misfortune—was the scion of a very humble family indeed, and his immediate progenitor had kept a small public-house in the suburbs of London. In front of the door was then situated a little common with a pond and a few gorse bushes, and on the common used to graze a donkey which seemed to be the property of the residents in general. On this donkey young Jones—who had not then blossomed into McCawmee—would vault, and seating himself on the extreme verge of the precipice bounded by the donkey's tail, would perform a series of unrivalled feats in the ring for the benefit of a very ragged circle of admirers. Mr. Jones, senior, died, as also perhaps the donkey—for the myth as to the immortality of these patient slaves lacks confirmation—the common became gradually absorbed into bricks and mortar, and Mrs. Jones with her family sought a new home. Young Jones (now McCawmee) had passed through many vicissitudes, and hitherto had derived neither pleasure nor profit from the talent on which he had once so prided himself. But everything comes to him who waits, and all knowledge will come in useful one day. There was considerable difference, no doubt, between riding on a bare-backed donkey and going a-hunting in fashionable guise, and in a position which he was now to assume for the first time. A little knowledge, however—the proverb notwithstanding—is better than none at all.

Almost immediately on his reappearance the horses were brought round, and the ordeal of mounting had to be gone through. The Squire lifted Maggie into her saddle, and then kept a furtive eye on Mr. Jones, who had tempered his valour at the last with a little discretion, and made up his mind that nothing should induce him to wear spurs. Even the donkey, he felt sure, would have rebelled against spurs, and no doubt if anything could have determined the old hunter that he was on the point of bestriding to be even less than usually energetic, it was the knowledge that the only stimulant to which he was accustomed to pay attention was on the present occasion absent. " The Boy "—the appellation had as little to do with age as formerly when applied to " post-boys " of mature years—was not long in making the discovery, as the clumsy way in which the new proprietor mounted would have been found exceedingly irritating had his heels been armed according to custom. As Mr. Jones scrambled into his seat, " The Boy " pricked up his ears as if asking, " Who have we here ? "

The Squire's face wore a puzzled look of amuse-

ment. Had he made a mistake? Could any one
come to grief on "The Boy"? If any one could
the very man was there now, and he, the Squire,
would have neglected the duties of a host. "I don't
know about that though," he said to himself. "Do
him good, perhaps. Take him down a peg. After
all the fellow's got some pluck. Or is it conceit?
Anyhow, I wish we were safe home again."

The meet was at a distance of about four miles
from the Hall. Jogging along quietly Mr. Jones
found but little difficulty in keeping his seat.
Rising in his saddle, as he saw the Squire do, was
hard work, but on the whole he had had no idea
that riding—as distinguished from donkey-riding—
was so easy. How absurd to keep people in riding-
schools for months. But his might be an exceptional case. It was a great thing, he felt, to be able
to ride. It was too ridiculous of those people who
criticized things they know nothing about. He
flattered himself that he had never—that he recol-
lected—written a book—or even greatly reviewed
one—on fox-hunting. It was a fortunate circum-
stance, and the more so that there was hardly any
other subject on which the world had not had the
benefit of his ideas. Now if there was a new series
of the Badminton Library, he would feel capable of

giving his opinion. He was immensely exhilarated
by the steady motion of "The Boy," and but that he
had a slight and unaccustomed feeling of modesty,
would have given vent to his excitement in a view-
halloo. But no doubt the Squire would consider this
in his department; and at all events it would be
well to wait awhile and hear how it was done.

The party of three had now reached a large
common, on one side of which was a ragged patch
or two of gorse, and the hounds were seen approaching along a road which intersected it. From every
side horsemen were arriving in every possible dress
—with the exception possibly of red-striped knickerbockers—and mounted on every conceivable variety
of the equine race. There were a few fashionables
in pink; some neatly attired, like the Squire, in
black; then the local horse-dealers and publicans, a
farmer or two, all the butchers of the neighbourhood
—how country butchers who only kill a sheep or
two a week can afford to live so merrily is a puzzle—
three or four boys, on ponies, who would go at
everything and somehow get over, and the usual
sweep. About half-a-dozen ladies were out, and
with two or three of these Maggie seemed to be
very friendly. There was soon quite a little group
of Dianas, one of them middle-aged and the re-

mainder too plain and too badly mounted to enter
into any sort of competition with Maggie. The
ladies one and all took the greatest interest in Mr.
McCawmee Jones—who had arrested his steed at a
convenient distance, as if to assist the photographers
—and those who were so fortunate as to possess
eye-glasses turned them on him without delay.

"Who is that, Maggie?" asked Mrs. Mumford, the
wife of a neighbouring squire. "I never saw him
before. I cannot congratulate you on your new
beau, if you intend that he shall pilot you."

"Oh, Mrs. Mumford, how can you!" replied
Maggie, blushing—as indeed she was accustomed
to do on very slight provocation. "He is a friend of
papa's. I believe he is a great writer and reviewer,
and so I should advise you to mind what you are
doing. We have two men staying with us. The
other, a cousin of papa's, Mr. Corthee, is just driving
up in the pony-carriage. He wouldn't ride. There
was old Harkaway for him if he had wished, but
perhaps he was wise not to venture. He is a poet,
and Mr. Jones is his friend" ("A very convenient
arrangement," put in Mrs. Mumford); "and if you
look your best there is no saying how famous he will
make you."

"Maggie will look her best now," said a tall, thin

girl, mounted on a raw-boned chestnut, as she pointed with her whip to a young man in pink who had just ridden up on a slashing thoroughbred bay horse, and was exchanging greetings with the Squire. "Now we can break up this little meeting, I suppose. I am going to speak to——" and without finishing her sentence she walked her horse towards another group, with whom she appeared to be on equally good·terms. Poor Maggie was blushing again. The young man on the bay was evidently coming nearer, though his approach was made so circuitously as to seem, to a careless glance, accidental. Just as he came within a yard or two, and had taken off his hat, the master gave the signal to throw off. The little group of Maggie's friends had melted away as if by magic, and she and the new-comer were riding together towards the covert on one side of the common which was to be first drawn. The man on the bay was a tall, broad, sufficiently good-looking young fellow. He did not appear to have many words to throw away, and as yet he had merely made a remark as to the point where the fox, which the hounds were certain to find, was likely to break covert. Maggie assented without a word, and indeed she could scarcely have taken the opinion of one better qualified to judge. Together they moved

towards the point indicated. A good number of the
field seemed to mistrust this judgment, or they may
have had other reasons for preferring a different course.
On witnessing the departure of the hounds the Poet
—who was shivering in his furs, and who had no one
to talk to, and would not have talked in any case—
giving a peevish and dissatisfied glance around,
requested the groom to drive him back to the Hall,
feeling that he had sufficiently studied the noble
sport of fox-hunting. He had also a second reason
for hurrying away. His idea of making love was
to retire to his room, and thence indite a sonnet
to his mistress's eyebrow, instead of wasting the
precious hours in her company. He had never been
smitten so hard before, and was fearful that the
feeling might evaporate, and with the feeling would
go the chance of gaining for himself on this occasion
the immortality he desired. An ancient might have
wished rather to immortalize Maggie.

Mr. Jones, at the moment when the hounds moved
off towards the covert, had found himself left alone.
The Squire was talking to a friend at a little
distance, and he felt at a loss how to proceed. The
new feeling was not particularly welcome. Mr.
Jones had about the average amount of courage, but
no amount of courage can supply the want of a little

experience. "The Boy" had been standing perfectly still, but his rider was not so simple as to imagine that this pleasing state of affairs was likely to continue. He was a witness of the arrival of the young man on the bay, and the sight of his perfect seat, and of the composed way in which he managed his spirited steed, gave him a new sensation almost akin to envy.

While almost every virtue has its drawbacks, there are faults and even vices which are not without their special advantages. The special advantage of conceit is that the owner is seldom troubled by envy. Whether it was the country air or not, Mr. Jones was regretfully conscious of feeling less conceited than usual, and therefore more inclined to envy. When the young man on the bay had made his discreetly circuitous approach to Maggie, Mr. Jones not only felt envious but jealous. Jealousy is the most pronounced form of envy. He had been immensely taken with his fair hostess, and the half-jocose intention that he had promulgated on the eve of leaving town in the Poet's chambers, was in process of developing. He—like the Poet—had been smitten over-night, and the sight of the charming nymph in her habit this morning had scarcely had the effect of healing the wound. Perhaps he was as much urged

on by the glances of annoyance which the Poet had
shot at him as by any shafts from Maggie's sparkling
eyes. He was conscious and felt proud of a rebellious
spirit which incited him to rise in arms against one
whose humble slave he had hitherto thought it no
shame to be considered. The advent of the young
man on the bay had the effect, notwithstanding
his inexperience, of determining him to great deeds.
Maggie should at least see that he was not afraid.
He would do or die. He forgot for the moment that
he did not know what to do or where to die. While
pondering these things with loose rein and knees far
from the saddle, he was conscious of a stir around
him. He heard a noise as of a dog baying or
whimpering. More dogs joined in. There was a
cry, a holloa of some sort ("Somebody is hurt,"
thought Mr. Jones), and suddenly "The Boy" faced
about and moved off at a trot. His rider looked up
just in time to see the young man on the bay push
his hat down firmly on his head, gather his reins
together, put spurs to his horse, and disappear gaily
over a fence which ran level with the boundary of
the covert. While Mr. Jones was congratulating himself on the disappearance of his rival, a horn was
blown somewhere in his immediate neighbourhood.
A second more and Maggie had popped over the

fence in the wake of the young man on the bay. There are a few moments in one's lifetime when one has to make up one's mind quickly. or be left behind. It must remain for ever uncertain what course Mr. Jones, if left to himself, would, in his utter ignorance, have determined on. But " The Boy " took the decision upon himself. He had been quiet as a lamb till the well-known sounds proclaimed that the hounds had found, and, almost immediately after, that the fox had "gone away." He then declined to stand still any longer. Indeed, it would have been impossible to make him understand that anything could be desired of him but to follow the hounds at his best pace. The old horse may have been aware that his pace was not what it had been, and that therefore it behoved him not to lose the start. He had indeed been all the time watching Maggie's pony, rightly judging that its rider would be more capable of deciding on a fit moment than his own. As Maggie put her pony—it was only a pony in name, and quite able to carry her safely anywhere —at the fence, the old horse got quietly into his stride and proceeded to follow. It would have required a stronger hand than Mr. Jones's to check him, if indeed any one could have done so. But it is exceedingly doubtful whether the Critic made any such attempt. It is even possible that his heroic mind may have scorned the idea of being left behind. Down came• "The Boy" to the fence, which was not such a very big one after all. Steadying himself without any help or hindrance from his rider, he took off in exactly the right place, landed well in the next field, and proceeded to do his best to overhaul Maggie and the young man on the bay.

It was a long time, so long a time indeed that the old horse had very likely forgotten it, since he had enjoyed a gallop under similar circumstances. He swerved, he capered like a colt with delight. There was that abominable saddle with the stirrups swinging about, and these useless reins threatening to get round his legs and throw him down ; but what did they matter ? For the first time for years he had got rid of his incubus. He was too sportsmanlike an old horse to have done so purposely, but the incubus had got rid of itself. In fact, Mr. Jones had been left behind, and was now rising from the ground with a crushed hat, a bruised shoulder, and sensations the reverse of triumphant. He had got down to the fence all right. When the horse rose in the air his rider had risen higher and higher with a forward movement, leaving the saddle below and behind him. Passing high over his horse's head he described a somersault in front of his steed, to that animal's temporary perplexity. But "The Boy" was as clever as a cat, and the Squire's confidence had been fully justified. As Maggie was preparing to take the next fence, she heard a sound of galloping in the rear, and "The Boy's" head appeared at her girths. To her no great surprise she saw that he was riderless. They took the fence together, "The Boy" keeping well out of her way. Then he kicked up his heels gaily, as if rejoicing in his freedom, and went on alone in pursuit of the hounds.

84

CHAPTER IX.

A CRITICAL DISCUSSION.

THE Squire and his daughter rode home together,
having been relieved of all anxiety on Mr. Jones's
account by the report of an eye-witness, who had
seen him starting for home on Shanks's mare. " The
Boy" could be trusted to find his way back to his
stables. On their arrival at the Hall they found
Mr. Jones waiting to receive them, wearied and sore
from the unaccustomed experience, and from having
had to walk home in boots at least a size too small
for him, but in the best possible spirits, and feeling
more or less of a hero. The Poet, who had spent
the afternoon in smoking endless cigarettes and in
searching for more than usually delusive rhymes,
was looking decidedly bilious. The Poet's admirers
were of opinion that the great man's genius was
never more apparent or, they added, more disagree-

able than when he was bilious. Maggie came down
to afternoon tea in a tea-gown which made her
look more charming than ever. But the fact was
that the dress she happened to be wearing was
always the dress in which you thought she looked
best, and in which you fancied you had wished to
see her. The Poet, who had never yet been really
in love, though he had written some reams concerning that passion, and who had not come down to
the country to waste his time, had scarcely finished
his first cup of tea before he yielded himself a
calculating captive. His way of showing his devotion
was so peculiar that his secret was likely to be well
kept. He had great belief in the theory of the
power of the human eye, and he laid himself out to
dominate Maggie as if he were some sort of beast-
tamer. To whatever part of the room he wandered
he kept his eye fixed, as far as possible, on his
"study." This made it necessary for him sometimes
to twist his neck like a corkscrew. It did not need
any peculiar power in the operator to make this
procedure very unpleasant for the victim. Poor
Maggie was speedily aware of the inspection to which
she was being subjected, but which it was impossible
to evade. Whenever she raised her eyes they were
encountered by the basilisk glance of the Poet,

sometimes standing near her, and as often scowling from afar off. She was talking to Mr. Jones, who had been assisting her in the duties of the tea-table, and whom conscious heroism had led to discard his usual affectations. Mr. Jones had been recounting his day's experiences. These; though the common lot of novices in the hunting-field, he seemed to consider truly exceptional. Probably Maggie had never heard the sensations of a novice, who has had a "cropper," and walked home afterwards in tight boots, described by one with such a flow of words. As the narrator would possibly have put it—if he, Mr. Jones, had not a flow of words, then who had ? She felt amused—more than amused, interested. Who could help liking the man who laughed so cheerily at his own misfortunes, which he owned were brought about by his own ignorance ? Mr. Jones had the less difficulty in confessing his ignorance on the recent occasion, as he certainly never intended after this evening to own to any want of knowledge or experience in sporting affairs. Probably Maggie was unaware how sympathizing she looked, or even how greatly a little sympathy increases, in the eyes of the fortunate object, the effect of charms which were potent enough before. The effect on Mr. Jones of her sympathy was soon

apparent. His great eyes—gooseberry, not blue, as
were the orbs of Mr. Corthee—began to seek hers
with an expression so absurdly tender that she was
at her wits' end to keep from laughing. The worst
of it was that if she turned away her eyes from one
admirer they encountered the moody glance of the
other, who was quickly adding to his stock-in-trade
a comprehension of the feeling of jealousy. Each
rival was thinking to himself, in a different way,
"The girl would do." Each was mentally confound-
ing "that other fellow"; but while the Poet thought
it the height of presumption for his friend to aspire,
the latter could not, even while entering his seventh
heaven, absolve himself from a charge of rebellion.
It was a relief to Maggie, at all events, when the big
bell announced that dinner would be served in half-
an-hour. The Poet hastened off to revel in what he
was accustomed to call "the pangs of love." It is
to be hoped that he found the reality enjoyable. He
raved about his room, taking long strides, and stopping
in the corners to twirl his moustache, and mouth a
line or two of what—perhaps from the absence of
the context—sounded very much like nonsense
verses. But he was no doubt happy in his misery.
So happy, indeed, that it was not until the bell
proclaimed dinner was ready that he threw himself

wildly into his clothes, and rushed into the drawing-room to find the Squire standing on the hearthrug, watch in hand, and looking exceedingly hungry.

The Poet was at first greatly disgusted to find that three guests had arrived, of whose expected presence he felt, in his new *rôle* of prospective son-in-law, he ought to have been informed. But a glance at the new-comers speedily reassured him. Two of these were the parson and his wife, while the third was the young man who had joined Maggie at the meet. The Poet did not recognize him, and indeed he looked a very different person on foot and in dress clothes. He was now heavy-looking and rather plain, but with a healthy fresh colour and a look of straightforward good-nature. Not the sort of young man—so thought the Poet—whom Maggie might be expected to care for. Mr. Jones had been a witness to the way in which Maggie had been appropriated directly the fox broke covert, and had an uneasy conviction that what had been done so naturally had been done often before. The parson was delighted, he said, to have the pleasure of meeting two such eminent literary notabilities. He did not add that the greater part of his enjoyment was derived from his intention to expose them.

Mrs. Butler was a worthy old lady, well up in soups and jellies, but with hardly an idea outside the parish. Both Poet and Critic were surprised no less than comforted to find that the young man, who was introduced as Mr. Charles Lovibond, did not appear anxious to attach himself on this occasion to Maggie. Perhaps it was only his slyness, yet he did not look very sly. The visitors speedily set him down as a nonentity. Mr. Jones, indeed, looked at him without feeling in the least moved to employ any of his usual flattery. But even the least valuable of pearls must not be too carelessly thrown away. As the art of flattery consists chiefly in praising people for good qualities most conspicuous by their absence, Mr. Jones, if he had chosen to flatter young Lovibond, would have complimented him on his intellectual appearance. A lover endows the object of his affections with the qualities he considers most desirable—probably with his own. Neither Maggie nor Mr. Lovibond would have cared much for the praises of which they were for different reasons deprived. Maggie's awe was in a state of suspension. Mr. Jones had shown that he could converse somewhat after the manner of an ordinary being; and Mr. Corthee had not yet given any proof that he was an extraordinary one. A woman's first

impressions of a man generally require considerable
correcting. Too frequently under the polished
exterior of the new idol lurks something rough
and distasteful; as often there is nothing under it
at all. One day there is a crash. She rises startled
from her knees, rubs her eyes, and transfers her
worship to another—and perhaps even yet another
—idol.

Dinner was announced; the Squire of course took
charge of Mrs. Butler, and—the parson withdrawing
good-naturedly in favour of the younger man—
Maggie fell once more to the lot of the Poet. Mr.
Jones took the seat on her other side; the parson
neighboured the Poet; while young Lovibond was
located between Mr. Jones and Mrs. Butler. The
Squire at once plunged into an animated conversation
on village matters with the parson and his wife,
which had been interrupted a fortnight ago. The
parson's eye, however, might be seen occasionally
to glance towards his left-hand neighbour, as if he
was fretting at the necessary postponement of the
promised encounter. Once or twice he addressed
a remark to the Poet, of which the latter took very
little notice. Maggie got tired of Mr. Corthee's
silence, and once more engaged Mr. Jones, who was
nothing loth,' in conversation. Mr. Lovibond had

often dined at the Hall before, but had never found the society so uncongenial. Cut off from Maggie, to whom he could have talked for ever about hunting, and from the Squire, with whom he had many interests in common, he listened with wonder and disgust to the well-modulated and perpetual flow of Mr. McCawmee Jones's small-talk. What on earth, he thought, was it all about? Not being able to answer the query, he resigned himself—for he had an excellent appetite—to his dinner.

The Poet worked the eye that was nearest to Maggie so hard that he almost developed a squint. But Maggie's face was averted. The soft murmur of Mr. Jones's meaningless nothings came to him like the humming of bees. He leant forward a little to listen.

"But you critics," Maggie was saying in her clear voice, "are very cruel, are you not? I wonder you can say such unkind things—of people you know too." Maggie's ideas of critics were rather old-fashioned. She had heard of Keats. "'Who killed John Keats?' 'I,' said the *Quarterly*,' etc." But Mr. Jones hastened to reassure her. The successor of Jeffrey was conscious of feeling anything but cruel. What he would have called "the sweet propinquity," to say nothing of a good dinner, made

him feel like a very good fellow indeed. Maggie
was an "outsider," and confession, which might ease
his soul, would go no further.

"We are awful humbugs now-a-days," he said,
with his oily smile. "I am afraid we have got into
the other extreme, and praise a great deal too indiscriminately. The fact is, if you won't praise, you
had better hold your tongue. A literary paper that
'slated' everybody would have but a brief existence,
since the only people likely to read it would be
authors searching for praise. Praise may not be as
as good as pudding, but it sometimes brings it, and
if not it is the next best thing. To get praise you
must praise other people. Then, too, we successful
literary men—I mean literary men who are reaping
their reward in shape of a return of praise—are but
a small band. United we stand, divided we fall.
It is a duty to uphold those who have been lucky
enough or clever enough to become members. I
said the band is a small one, but it is quite large
enough, and if any critic is now-a-days so cruel as to
blackball a candidate, it is because he thinks there
is no more room. As it is, some of the old members
get little enough to eat, and new members are apt
to be ravenous. It sounds bad, doesn't it? but we
are not altogether humbugs; there is so much we

can honestly praise. Oh, so much. Our friend there"—with a jerk of his fork, which had been conveying some candied fruit to his mouth, in the direction of the Poet—"is unutterably sweet." Mr. Jones kept up his own supply of sweetness by swallowing a large candied apricot.

"Do you honestly think," inquired Maggie, "that there are modern poets who equal the old? Papa and Mr. Butler won't allow it for a moment. Papa has an admirable collection of old poets, but no moderns at all. You think he ought to get some?"

"Well," returned the Critic dubiously, "it is not for me to say. If you ask my candid opinion, between ourselves I don't know that a collection of our modern poets will be greatly valued by posterity. But we do not live for posterity any more than for the generations that are gone by. I confess I prefer the ancients myself, only I mustn't say so. There would be very poor pickings to be got by criticizing the ancients, who, you are aware, have already undergone the process."

Maggie was here aware of a slight movement on her other side, as of the Poet pricking up his ears. Her fine eyes opened wider, her lower lip pouted as if with vexation.

"You are joking, of course, Mr. Jones," she said; "you clever people think, I suppose, that we country-folk are only fit to be made fun of."

"Mr. Jones is telling me," she said, addressing herself to the Poet, "that the critics we have been taught to believe in are sheer humbugs, that he is as bad as the rest, and that if they did not praise people indiscriminately they would have to give up business. I suppose he is joking, but what am I to believe? If they praise people they do not believe in, they are not only humbugs themselves, but they are foisting shame on us."—Archly, "Does Mr. Jones praise you much?"

The Poet had no sense of humour, and he proceeded to answer his questioner in all seriousness.

"I know nothing about critics, Miss Ellis—as critics, that is: privately, of course, I know one or two. I should prefer they should leave my writings alone, but what can I do? Fame has its drawbacks. I know Mr. Jones as a clever man, whose opinions on art and poetry are infallible, and always sweetly expressed."—"Sweet, sweet, sweet," thought Maggie, who was here sensible of a movement as of the Critic pricking up his ears.—"Not that I look up to them myself, but——"

Maggie at this moment caught the eye of Mrs. Butler, and rose rather hastily from her seat. Mr. Lovibond rose too, and moved to the door more rapidly than could have been expected. In another moment the ladies were gone.

CHAPTER X.

THE RECTOR ON POETS AND POETRY.

MAGGIE went back to the drawing-room feeling
puzzled and disturbed in her ideas. Truth to say,
she had looked forward with more interest than she
had herself been aware of to the temporary lighting
up of her calm and rather dull life by the two—as
she had figured them—brilliant literary luminaries.
She had been tolerably content hitherto with her
surroundings, and indeed had of late been trying to
convince herself that she had no sufficient reason for
grumbling with the lot which appeared to have been
provided. But most of us are able on occasion to
recognize the fact that we are a little thrown away,
and she had not been without visions of the possibility of something brighter interposing. It appeared
then that her father had been right. The modern
literary man, if these were average specimens, was
indeed a descent from those of the past. She was

however too sensible not to be aware that the data
on which to form a sweeping judgment were absurdly inadequate. She sighed, but not very deeply
—Mrs. Butler was arranging herself comfortably
with a view to "forty winks"—and proceeded with
the arrangement of a harmless little plot which had
struck her as likely to detect the impostors, if such
indeed they were. She went to a cabinet standing
in a corner of the room, and brought thence a
number of small volumes containing selections of
the poets she had been taught most to revere.
Placing these treasures on the table, she covered
them with some worsted-work—if a clever woman
can once make you believe in her simplicity, all's
over with you—and sat down to await the course of
events. When the gentlemen came in she would
turn the conversation to her favourites. If the
new-comers sneered at them, if the modern Poet
in fact did not acknowledge the supremacy of his
teachers, or those who ought to have been so, she
would know what to think. She recurred to her
father's idea of a competition between the old and
the new, and saw that it might be productive of
more than amusement. She imagined that she had
seen something in the face of the Poet which suggested that he had sufficient conceit not to shrink

from the ordeal. She passed rapidly over in her mind a few of the poems which have stirred men's— and women's—hearts for ages, and wondered what Mr. Corthee would have to show against these. That ridiculous Critic—whom she rather liked— would it be possible for him, after his recent confession, to support his friend ? It was a question whether a man who owned to imposture could rightly be called a humbug.

No doubt there are women who look their best when there is no male creature present to admire. Of these Maggie may have been one. She certainly looked very lovely as she stood—her preparations over—with her lips parted in a dubious smile. Her pleasure was enhanced, as whose is not, by the doubt whether the promised sport was not a little —just a little—improper or unkind.

Immediately on her leaving the dining-room the Squire had moved to his daughter's seat at the top of the table, and the parson had drawn his chair closer to the Poet. The latter saw himself hemmed in not without suspicion, and retreated at once as much farther as possible into his shell. Mr. Jones scented an engagement, to the prospect of which, in Maggie's absence, he was anything but averse. He prepared for battle by stripping himself rapidly of the encumbrance of his recently-expressed sincerity, and putting on once more the false self which had got to be almost the true one. He felt like a child who, while well aware that the house of cards he has constructed with much labour is but a poor edifice, yet resists any attempt at knocking it down. Had Maggie remained he might have been a traitor —and true. What a predicament the Poet would have found himself in! since the presence of Maggie would also have inspired the "old fogies," who appeared already sufficiently eager for the fray. He could hardly have told how he knew that the Squire and the parson were thirsting, metaphorically, for his blood. "Who is this old parson?" Mr. Jones was saying to himself; "he looks like somebody, and yet I never heard of him. I am afraid he is going to talk. I would give something to be safe in the drawing-room."

Not a word had passed between the two allies, though Mr. Jones had intercepted a rapid glance from the parson to his host, which the clever observer had interpreted to mean, "Let me begin." Very little time was lost in beginning.

"So we are honoured, in these wilds, by a visit from a new poet," said Mr. Butler, in his politest tones, through which was yet noticeable a faint trace of old-fashioned sarcasm. " The honour is a great one indeed. We are not so distant or so deaf but that we have heard the flourish of trumpets. I am old enough to have heard flourishes which have heralded nothing. Don't imagine I am suggesting that yours could be a case of that sort. But we old fogies grow sceptical. For my part I can only wonder. There were surely poets enough, and some of them not very bad ones. One or two even whom it would be hard to surpass. I own I am a stickler for content. When you have a good thing, why not rest and be thankful ? You remember the lines—

'Dost thou laugh to see how fools are vexed
  To add to golden numbers golden numbers ? '

Was there ever yet a time which gained anything by the variations of nimble professors ? But you will despise me for talking about things I confess to being ignorant of. Your muse and I must be better acquainted."

The Poet leant back in his chair, his head thrown back, and his long thin greyish locks floating out behind him. As he watched the smoke curl up from the end of his cigarette, his expression was as of one undergoing physical pain. He was indeed thinking that of all bores he had met, the literary-clerical promised to be the worst. He had never undergone this particular torture before, and did not care to hide the fact that he was annoyed while protesting by his manner that he was superior to it. There was nothing in the parson's words which an ordinary man might not have taken good-temperedly. Princes, it must be remembered, are precluded from descending into the arena. He looked appealingly towards Mr. Jones, as in olden times an insulted and not too patient baron might have motioned to the first and second murderers, " Despatch me, I prithee, this troublesome blade ; " and the Critic, as in duty bound, lost no time in responding after his modern manner.

"Surely," he lisped, with a show of more than his usual deference, and leaning forward a little in his chair, "there have been a few discoveries and inventions in the world since the days of—shall we say Shakespeare ? Why should we rule that poetry is to be the only thing that is to remain without improvement, and, according to your view, not even *in statu quo ?* I cannot see why, with modern advantages and the increase of knowledge, we should not be able to turn out as good work as the men of the past. Our friend here "—pointing his fork (with which he was now conveying an olive to his mouth) at the Poet—" has certainly produced some things

which are very sweet. If he will allow me to say so"
—the Poet made the usual slight gesture of dissent
—" some things which are inexpressibly sweet."

This was in Mr. Jones's usual style of criticism.
"This poet," he would say of a new client, "has
made an unsurpassed bid for immortality"; or,
"To-day it is our happy lot to inscribe a new name on
the roll of fame"; or, "For sweetness these poems are
absolutely unrivalled"—till next week. Of course,
when it was stated that they were "inexpressibly
sweet," no one could be disappointed at not hearing
wherein the special sweetness lay.

Mr. Jones eat his olive, while the parson struck in
again—

"Of course I am not so silly as to think that no
one now writes good verses or good prose, or even
that occasionally some one does not hit on a new
idea, or at all events on an idea that the majority
think new. But I think the some one very lucky
to hit on it, and doubly lucky not to be found out.
I am afraid that research has, to a great extent,
taken the place of originality. No doubt it is better
to be able to resuscitate, alter, or adapt what had
slipped into oblivion than to do nothing at all.
Modern poets have so many examples to study
from that bad work would be as inexcusable as

turning out a bad steam-engine. There is a good deal of the mechanic about your poet now-a-days. Of the old poets, Tom Moore (whose lyrics are wonderfully good, considering that he wrote with a purpose) is the only one that I can remember who ever suggested a mechanical invention. It is now pretty well known that he invented—on paper— switchback railways. A modern engineer is rather an improver than an inventor. With all his improvements he has not been able within the last thirty years to increase very much, if at all, the speed on railways. Poetry rather demands an inventor than an improver. No amount of work or of polishing will make up for the withdrawal of the 'divine *afflatus*.' You cannot take other people's poetry and improve it as you would a steam-engine ; nor can you begin again and invent steam. Clever people discover in old libraries and odd corners—you could find no end of them here—things that have been forgotten, or perhaps were never known to more than a few, and perhaps are not even good. The digging out and polishing up of these is a praiseworthy employment, not so the presenting them in a slightly altered setting as their own. I pity people who must write—only I don't see why they must—they are so heavily handicapped by the

enormous amount that has been already written.   If
they read much they cannot be original.   They get
steeped to the lips in old literature, and out of the
abundance they speak.   On the other hand, if they
read little or nothing, they say things which have
been said before, and resemble a man hurrying off to
the Patent Office with an invention which he should
have known was patented a hundred years ago."

Perhaps the parson was rather too evidently
enjoying himself.   It is sufficiently aggravating to
be flogged without having to bear in addition the
self-congratulatory looks of the clever performer.
As a Don the parson had had frequent opportunities
of laying down the law.   These were now valued in
proportion to their rarity.   He really believed there
were no modern poets.   The belief, at any rate,
absolved him for his ignorance.   The Squire looked
round as to say, " You hear that.   How do you like
it ? "   Young Lovibond had at the tip of his tongue
a remark on the day's hunting which had been
suggested by the parson's mention of " digging out,"
but he was a slow speaker, and before he was ready
the Critic's unctuous voice was heard again.   The
turn of affairs was not pleasing to the Londoners,
who were of the class who wish to talk or not to
talk, as the case may be, but have a standing

objection to being talked to. "He will be starting again," Mr. Jones had thought, "unless I cut in."

"There are moderns," he observed, à *apropos* of nothing, "who write admirable plays."

"Are there ?" said the parson quickly. "I am indeed happy to hear it. I should be happier if you could tell me why they write them. Are they likely to improve on Shakespeare, who, though few know him well, is just well enough known for it to be almost impossible to crib from him. To be a third-rate Shakespeare would be no doubt to prove oneself of—in these days—exceptional talent, but after that—of what possible use would a third-rate Shakespeare be to me ? "

" If every one was judged by your standard," said Mr. Jones suavely, " there would be little room for mediocrity. But it seems to me that an indiscriminate admiration for old poets commits you to worshipping a host of inferiors. There are numbers of poets (and others) who, because they happened to write fairly well in days when few people wrote any better, have got, so to speak, bound up with fame, and thus have an immortality of stupidity. They are 'standard works' because they crept into this collection or that. People—who do not read them— talk about them as if they ought to be read. And there are others who long ago hit the popular fancy, or what answered in those days to the popular fancy, in whom educated men can now see little or nothing to admire, and whom we indeed consider over-rated." (The Squire, who, having seen the discussion well started, had begun to nod, sat bolt upright in his chair.) " You would not I suppose forbid the moderns to compete with them ? "

" Over-rated ! " exclaimed the parson.

" You've said it now," murmured young Lovibond enthusiastically.

"Over-rated!" said the Squire, shaking off his disposition to slumber. "I am delighted that a Londoner can see what a shameful state of affairs we suffer from. I should think, indeed, that we are over-rated. Little do townsfolk imagine the burdens that land has to bear. My poor farmers, what with School-board rates, tithes—one for you, parson—highways, County Councils, and a score of things besides, are being ruined as fast as possible. Now we are to have the Small Holdings Act on the top of it all, and up will go rates again. When the best land has been taken for these fellows (whoever they are to be, and who will never make it pay), the farmers, who can't make a living as it is, are to subsist on the worst land. It is odd that the Tory party don't see that the agricultural interest

can't go on unless something is done soon. Surely
they don't fancy that creating sham yeomen is help-
ing the agricultural interest. Every now and then
a vote-hunting Radical comes down and shows us
what miserable beings we are, and how we have to
bear up the whole country. Atlas was nothing to it.
But of course we can't admit to Radicals that everything is not just as it should be, seeing that our own
friends did not help us when they got the chance.
It is all 'the working-man' now. I am sick of him,
for my part, and should think he must be sick of
being buttered." ("People can stand a good deal of
butter," interrupted Mr. Jones.) "Now, if instead
of beginning at the wrong end the Government would
do something for my farmers so that they could do
something for the agricultural labourer, there would
be some sense in it. But then that would stop
agitation, which is the breath of life to some people.
Over-rated, indeed! By the bye, when we get into the
drawing-room, Maggie shall read you some verses—
I won't say poetry—on the state of rural affairs.
They were written by a friend of mine on one of our
farmers who went off to New Zealand the other day
—just one of those we ought to have kept at any
price."

The Poet was conscious of a suspicion that his

host was chaffing him. Had he come down into the country to hear other people's verses ? No one had ever dreamt of offering him such an indignity before. It had always been, "Oh, Mr. Corthee, that sweet thing of yours now—really too sweet." Even Mr. Jones glanced at the Squire with a polite air of deprecation. The latter discovered that something was wrong, and desisted, rather reluctantly, from his harangue. "Much these fellows care about the backbone of the country," he muttered—as if it was a case of lumbago. Aloud he said—

"Gentlemen, if no one will take any more wine, we will go into the drawing-room. Perhaps Mr. Corthee" —sarcastically—"will read us a poem or two. I am afraid I have been talking about things you do not understand. Now you can pay me out."

All rose with alacrity for various reasons. The Poet because he was bored, and because he hoped that he would soon have to refuse, unsuccessfully, to read his poems, and also because he thought it was time for his eye to be fixed on Maggie again; Mr. Jones was desirous of making love after a more ordinary fashion; the parson was anxious to bring his critical powers to bear on the poetry, as to the merits of which he had already made up his mind; the Squire had determined that Maggie should read the verses on the expatriated farmer; while young Lovibond was, to his surprise, conscious of feeling more than ordinary amusement. It was not perhaps as good as fox-hunting, but these fellows were really not bad sport.

" Hang it all, you know! By Jove! to look at that thin chap. He's a caution."

Mrs. Butler, hearing the footsteps of the approaching males, instinctively sprang up and arranged her cap; while Maggie removed herself from the neighbourhood of the mine to which some one would no doubt oblige her by applying a match.

CHAPTER XI.

AN INTERRUPTED COMPETITION.

ON arriving in the drawing-room the Poet at once looked out for a position whence to resume his dominating glances, to which the object's evident uneasiness gave additional zest. Mr. Jones walked up to Maggie and engaged her in conversation.

"We were having a discussion," he remarked suavely, "as was indeed to be expected. Perhaps I should rather say that Mr. Butler has been giving us a lecture. We finished by getting on to 'rates,' and there I felt like a fish out of water. Your father won't allow there are any living poets, and I am bound to differ from him. Oh!"—in answer to an upbraiding look—"I could not go so far as that, you know. Business is business. If you had been there I should have done my best to agree with you, no doubt; though to say there are no modern poets—actually none, you know—would be to pro-claim myself an ass."

While he spoke Maggie was being irresistibly attracted towards the table on which her little heap of books was arranged. Soon her hand was on the worsted-work with which the little battery was masked. The Critic was so used to all sorts of humbug and pretence, that he was able and some-times even too ready to detect it. It was child's play for him to discover, when Maggie glanced shyly up at him, that there was something under that worsted-work which she was half wishing to disclose and was yet desirous of hiding. What could the secret be? Possibly, nothing very important. Could Maggie have been writing poetry herself? Now he thought of it, she was just the sort of girl to write poetry—well, verses. After his frank con-fession in the dining-room it seemed not unlikely that she should wish to confide in him. If that was so, he smiled as he recognized that she need be in little fear of harsh judgment. She should be a poetess—a Laureatess—if she chose. Mr. Jones was one of those—of whom there are still a good many, and who must be obnoxious to every sensible girl—who, while thinking it a sacred duty to flatter a good-looking woman to the top of her bent, would never dream seriously of allowing that she had anything but her "charms"—as the Poet would have said—to recommend her. Strong-minded, plain women he hardly considered women at all, and he flattered them in quite a different way, which presumably—though there was a doubt about it—was what they wanted.

Having made up his mind as to the nature of the coming revelation, he fixed his eyes with all the eagerness of a terrier on the spot whence the secret might be expected to bolt. Maggie laughed nervously when the Critic calmly removed the worsted-work, and took in his hand the volume on the top of the little pile. His face fell as he recognized his mistake.

" Charming, delightful !" he exclaimed, with mock unction; "these are your favourites, Miss Ellis ? Very nice indeed," he continued, his manner getting more and more contemptuous, as one by one the collection passed through his hands. " Selections from Byron !"—in a surprised tone.

" Why not?" said Maggie, ready in a moment to take up the cudgels; "I have always understood that he was one of our great poets."

" Well, yes," said the Critic dubiously; "only I thought I had shown pretty conclusively that there was very little of the true poet about him.

He will never go down to posterity with our friend here. I wrote, indeed—but you may not have read it—that Byron was all fustian and bombast. Moreover, I offered to write a *Siege of Corinth* in four-and-twenty hours, which would be quick work. Byron! Really, Miss Ellis, your taste is a little antediluvian—from living in the country, no doubt. Byron, to put it vulgarly, is as dead as Julius Cæsar, I assure you. I fancy you would find a study of the moderns more improving than Byron, though, perhaps, not quite so amusing. Yet I would be generous. We can surely afford to be generous. For all that poor Byron is dead as Julius Cæsar, I will not deny that he may have written a good thing or two."

The Squire and the parson were bringing the reserves into action, the latter evidently with the intention of forcing the fighting, when the voice of young Lovibond was unexpectedly heard addressing the Poet. The young man had been thinking that he had acted a boorish part during dinner, and he did not wish " these Cockneys " to imagine that young fellows in the country were without an idea in their heads. In fact Mr. Lovibond had two— hunting and Maggie. He had been doubtful how best to open a conversation—for he was no great talker—when Mr. Jones's last words gave him his

I

cue. "Talking hunting, by Jove," he said to himself; "who'd have thought it?"

"We had a good thing to-day, if you like," he
began. "I did not see you out, but we got away so
quickly that I might have missed you. I hope you
were there"—to himself, "Gad! he doesn't look like
it"—"Saw your friend, though. I twigged the
Squire's old pink. There's a mulberry mark on the
left shoulder. A little tight for our friend, who looks
short of work. He came a cropper, I heard. Do
him a lot of good. We lost our fox at Bagnal Wood.
Ought to have killed. Do you know the country,
Mr.—Mr.——?"

The Poet stared at his interlocutor in blank
astonishment. Know the country, indeed! What
did this bumpkin mean? He knew as much as
he wanted to know about it, and the people too—
always excepting Maggie. "I dare say," he
replied rudely, "that I know as much about the
country Mr.—Mr.——as you know about the
town."

"You might easily know more," said young
Lovibond, nettled at the receipt of his advances
("Confounded bear," he muttered aside); and he
rapidly decided that he was unadapted by nature to
converse with a "Cockney." The parson caused a

welcome diversion. He was, indeed, burning to avenge Mr. Jones's disparaging mention of Byron.

"I can't imagine," he began, "why you literary men of the rising generation make such a dead set at Byron. I shall be exceedingly surprised—or my ghost—if one in a thousand of you will get a hundredth part of his lease of fame. I should call it 'fouling your own nest,' but that you are of the namby-pamby order—birds of quite another feather. In not showing appreciation of fire and feeling you commit yourselves, I suppose, to an opinion that poetry is possible without both or either. You won't find many to agree with you, but you are yourselves quite a little public. It is easy to exalt the indispensable art of manufacture and machinery too highly. Technical skill is all very well—I had been under the impression that Byron was not without skill—but what is mere skill in versifying without passion or fire, or whatever you choose to call them? —fustian and bombast! To me it seems childish to argue that any modern could have written *Childe Harold*. I will be silent about *Don Juan*, as I am, of course, not blind to its gross defects; yet parts of that poem have, in my opinion, never been equalled. Are none of Byron's lyrics the work of a true poet? Half-a-dozen of them would suffice to set up a modern poet in business. As for writing a modern *Siege of Corinth*, there is no objection surely to any one doing so who wishes, but what would be the good of it ? At best it could be but an impertinent imitation or parody, and of imitations I, for one, think we have had enough. A painter who is but a clever copyist is not, that I am aware of, considered a genius."

The Poet, having recovered his equanimity, was busily making a pretence of not listening to the harangue.

"I confess," put in the Squire, "that I know little or nothing about modern poetry—indeed, I have got to think there is none—but I am willing to be enlightened. I have a magnificent collection in my library of the rarest editions of almost every English poet from—from"—the Squire hesitated—"Adam to Byron, and I imagined that there was as little worth reading after the latter as—here, perhaps, Mr. Jones will agree with me—before the former. I may be wrong, of course. I ought to have bought my cousin Corthee's books—as he did not send them to me—but no doubt he has them with him. Maggie and I, and Mr. Butler also, I have no doubt,"—here the parson made a wry face,—"will have the greatest pleasure in listening to any new thing that you may think worthy of being put in competition with the old. But first I will ask Maggie to read the verses to which I referred just now." To Maggie—" My dear, where are those lines on poor Smout who went to New Zealand ? Our friends would like to hear them."

Maggie looked rather astonished, but after searching through a scrap-book on the table, soon came forward again with a slip of paper in her hand. The parson had no time to protest against what he thought an ill-advised interruption of the intended programme.

" You will read it, papa, I hope ? " said Maggie.

" Not I," said the Squire. " I can't read poetry— or verses. Read it yourself."

Maggie stood for a minute in silent protest with the slip of paper in her hand. She looked from one to the other. All, with the exception of the parson, seemed desirous that she should proceed. Her father because he really thought the verses very fine ; Messrs. Jones and Corthee because they hoped to find them very bad ; and young Lovibond because he had an idea that the reading of them would somehow " take the shine out of the Cockneys."

Maggie felt very shy, and she blushed of course ; but she was accustomed—when the doing so was not too disagreeable—to please others. She commenced reading in a low voice, which gradually gained confidence as she forgot her audience and only remembered poor Mr. Smout, who had had the Home Farm for many years, and who was now so many thousands of miles away. And this is what she read—

GONE TO NEW ZEALAND.

"Off to New Zealand yesterday;
   This was his only chance they told him;
He was a farmer, tradesmen they
   Accustomed to advise and scold him.
These glibly speed upon its way
   The lessening bark we sadly scan.
Wits miss their butt and rogues their prey,
   For us, we lose our honest man.

At least he soiled not England's name
   By arming 'gainst her breast her foes,
Or starving India made cry shame
   On rotten cloths and calicoes.
Let hungry placemen foul their nest
   And to debase their country vie,
But in his patriotic breast
   Their madness never found ally.

Though forced in self-defence to know
   The rudiments of many trades,
He lacked the polished swagger so
   Distinguishing commercial blades.
He could not pose in the *Gazette*
   'Midst giant sums which so astound,
Nor cleverly a fortune net
   To fail for twopence in the pound.

A Tory still, he could but tire
  Of those who 'in' forgot his need,
And 'out' his welfare must desire,
  But inability could plead.
While demagogues—which vexed his soul—
  As truer friends preferred loud claims,
And made him by each cunning dole
  Their stalking-horse to selfish aims.

His tithes he paid, yet wondered how
  The more corn fell the more they rose,
Since tithes repair no churches now
  Or warm poor parson's portless nose.
His roads untaxed trim bagmen ground,
  The lavish School-board learnt to cling
To his o'erloaded shoulders round,
  And made spoiled ploughboys sum and sing.

He toiled, made honey ; as it grew
  The drones rapacious filched his store
Before the taste himself he knew,
  Nor left him heart to gather more.
His ill-spared coin like drops of blood,
  His sweat ubiquitous o'erran
His parish with impartial flood,
  Or larded wastes of Hindoostan.

This couldn't last ; collectors call
  Too often at his surly door :
The world grew rich ; who bore it all
  —Atlas—grew thinner and more poor.
Friends whom his votes had helped to scale
  Life's ladder, pledges half outgrown
Took office, turned deaf ear, turned tail,
  Turned lords, and kicked the ladder down.

So wisely while he could he went,
　　The last of all we thought to spare,
· While some surviving coins unspent
　　In much-worn pocket lingered rare ;
Ere the poor 'guardian of the poor,'
　　Victim of fate's excessive whim,
Stood suppliant at the workhouse door,
　　Which sadly oped to welcome him."

Maggie's hand, with the paper in it, fell to her side. She turned away to replace the verses in the scrap-book.

"I call that good," said the Squire aggressively, "considering that it is modern, and does not pretend to be poetry."

"That's all nonsense about tithes growing larger," objected the rector. "My tithes are down to nothing. Why couldn't the fellow stick to his facts?"

"Excellently read," said the Critic, glad to have it over.

The Poet saw that to raise a discussion on such trumpery was to defer the introduction of more interesting matter. "You don't call it poetry," he said carelessly, and as if he felt thereby absolved from further criticism.

The Squire accepted the situation rather sulkily, but a debate cannot be sustained against the silence of the opposition benches.

"I told you it was not what you call poetry, only a versified statement of the position of rural affairs. I should beg your pardon for introducing such topics, but to us they are rather important. Now we can go back to what we were talking about. Byron was as dead as Julius Cæsar, and we were on the point, I fancy, of hearing who had superseded him. I am not too old to learn, or too conceited to confess my ignorance. I hope Mr. Corthee will not feel too bashful to enlighten our darkness, and, if we are no longer to worship our old idols, to show us a better religion."

The Squire sat down in his arm-chair with an air of resignation which suggested that he would sit there for a week if required.

Young Lovibond came up to the table with the air of one who anticipated and was even willing to assist in the production of a little amusement. The Poet was asking himself whether he would be worse in his jocose than in his polite mood. "Mr.—this gentleman," he went on, after once more trying to recall the Poet's name, and using the phraseology he was accustomed to employ at Conservative smoking concerts, "will kindly favour us with the next song."

"I am not in the habit of singing," said the Poet huffily; "nor do I generally"—he added, as if he was

a railway contractor—"carry my works about with
me. I am afraid"—and there is no doubt that he
felt genuine pity—"you must manage to put up for
to-night with Byron."

"I happen, by the merest chance," here put in the
Critic, who had before found it convenient to be able
in this way to assist a bashful client, "to have in my
pocket Mr. Corthee's last little book. Perhaps he
will read something"—the Poet waved a disclaimer
—"or I will, with his permission, read a little piece
or two which I think will put poor Byron into the
shade."

The Poet neither gave consent nor withheld it.
He certainly had the acquired faculty of looking
extremely bored.

A little circle formed round Mr. Jones, who took a
small book from the pocket of his dress-coat, opened
it, and held it out in his right hand, while with his
left he pawed the air like an impatient courser.
The Squire and the parson, notwithstanding the
former's declaration, exchanged a glance of triumph.
Surely the enemy was delivered into their hands.
Maggie became pleasingly sensible of the fact that
the Poet was no longer regarding her.

"It cannot be all nonsense," she was thinking,
"though he does not resemble my outward idea of

a poet. We shall have a treat, no doubt," and she composed herself to listen. She stood up facing the reader, her hands clasped behind her, her rosy lips parted in expectation. How foolish her own trifling rhymes would hereafter appear!

All at once she started. Young Lovibond, bent on improving the occasion, had stolen behind her, and, the scrutiny of the "Cockneys" being temporarily withdrawn, had taken her two hands in his own. What was she to do? She could not call out, and roughly to remove her hands from custody would make a scene. Certainly she did not wish to make a scene. She was not even quite clear that she would have objected to Tom Lovibond, one of her oldest friends, playing childish tricks—as indeed he was always doing. But she did not like it before these strangers. Gradually a blush stole down over her neck and bosom. When the Critic looked round to command attention, Mr. Lovibond, feeling rather foolish, moved away. Maggie felt that it was almost like sacrilege to be—foolish on an occasion like the present.

And now the voice of Mr. Jones was heard, sad, pathetic, with even an added wail of despair. He prided himself, not without reason, on his reading.

" And was it all you said ? "

He paused triumphantly and looked round.   It would have been wiser perhaps to go on.

"What an unnecessary question!" broke in the parson, with a short laugh.   "Surely he would have known—if he listened—whether he, or she (I suppose it is a she) said any more.   If there was no more, why ask ?   If any more was said we might have been told so without making a kind of riddle of it.   Perhaps after all it was sufficient; only we were talking of Byron.   He, I am sure, would not have asked such a question, though perhaps he might have pleaded—

> "'Oh, talk not to me.'"

"If you would have the goodness to wait," Mr. Jones was at last able to interpose, still holding the little book in his outstretched hand, "you would hear all about it.   It is surely absurd to criticize what you have not heard.   Allow me to proceed." And he began again.

> "And was it all you said ?
>   Salt tears, restrain your flow.
> No crystal drop be shed
>   Until the worst I know,
> That nothing more was said.
>
> If that was all you said——"

"If Peter Piper picked a peck of pepper," put in young Lovibond, who on this first and only occasion came forward as a critic of poetry. "Don't you know—couldn't you now find something a little livelier? That seems to me a trifle melancholy. Maggie—I mean Miss Ellis," he went on, struck by a bright idea, "won't you give us *John Peel?*"

"Do be quiet, Mr. Lovibond," said Maggie, who, whatever her disappointment, felt that politeness demanded the hearing of the precious specimen to the end. She had quickly decided that she would deny herself the satisfaction of submitting her effusions to the judgment of her guests.

It was probably a relief to every one when the Poet took the matter into his own hands. Walking up to Mr. Jones, he snatched the little book out of his hand and put it in his pocket.

"I'll wish you good-night," he said, moving towards the door; and without fulfilling this promise he speedily disappeared. Mr. Lovibond ordered his trap. All felt that the "competition" had been a failure—or rather that there had been none. As Maggie was saying "good-night" to Mr. Lovibond, he bent with a tragic air over her hand.

"'And was it all you said?'" he whispered in mock-heroic tones.

"It was a great deal too bad of you, Mr. Lovibond," said Maggie, trying to restrain a smile.

"Mr., indeed !" said he, dropping her hand, and making for the door.

Maggie looked after him thoughtfully. "He is certainly better," she said to herself, "than a score of these mock poets and sham critics. But then, that is not saying very much."

CHAPTER XII.

AT THE HOME FARM.

WHEN the Poet had taken his candle, together with his abrupt departure, he had been fully determined that on the next morning he would bid farewell to Beddington. He had never been so insulted before, and the Squire had evidently enjoyed the onslaught of that horrid parson. It was not, he thought, for himself that he complained, but for his art, which had been insulted through him. He would pack his things in the morning before breakfast. Jones, who was a regular trimmer, might do as he liked. The latter was welcome to Maggie, who, however, was evidently destined for that booby young squire. They would make a fine pair. The remembrance of young Lovibond's rude laughter came to him as a shock. He had no idea that such vulgar people existed. No doubt Maggie was as bad as the rest. Beautiful! oh, yes, she was beautiful—a blooming village hoyden—but it was scarcely the sort of beauty that a poet, or a modern poet at all events, should bow down to. Before he extinguished his candle, Mr. Corthee had quite convinced himself that the only type of beauty for which a poet should greatly long was the exact opposite to Maggie's. The form of a woman he knew, and whose talents he appreciated perhaps none the less that he imagined the feeling was returned, rose before him. A long thin face, its paleness slightly embrowned—or yellow. Eyes thoughtful, hair not too tidy, dress peculiar—how the Beddington folk would stare at it!—tastes literary, mind a little strong. Her image hovered over him, as he dozed off, bearing in one hand an enormous white lily. To the waving of this emblem sleep at last visited his eyelids.

On waking in the morning he did not at first remember either his over-night determination to quit Beddington, or his renunciation of Maggie. When they occurred to him he at once put the first on one side as foolish, since he had never yet packed his own things, and had a decided distaste to attempting it. Under the circumstances he could hardly summon Mr. Jones—who had recently been accustomed to "valet" him—to his aid. It would be better to swallow his annoyance, and defer his departure until the date originally fixed. As for Maggie, he quite forgot that he had renounced her at all. In reality he was conscious of something warmer than he was accustomed to feel at the knowledge that he would have another day of her sweet company. The word "sweet" occurred as frequently in the thoughts and language of Messrs. Jones and Corthee as in *Hymns Ancient and Modern.* Perhaps on this occasion the epithet was well applied.

As he descended to breakfast he was nourishing a feeling of anger against the Critic. He had for some time accustomed himself to look on him as an unswerving ally, but last night there had been symptoms of an intention to desert. The first whisper of rebellion rouses in the breast of the autocrat blind and unreasoning anger. It could not have been accident that had caused Mr. McCawmee Jones on the previous evening to make that foolish and fatal pause. He had wished, no doubt, to make him appear ridiculous in Maggie's eyes. It needed but the certainty of this to bring the Poet back to his allegiance. Whether he wanted Maggie or not, he would never yield her up to such an ass as Jones. Something too his eye-work must—if there was any faith to be placed in travellers' tales, and he forgot

K

that there is generally very little—have effected. As
he took his seat at the breakfast table, after saluting
his hostess, there was a look in his face which would
have told her—had she had the slightest idea that
she had offended him—that she was forgiven.

Far more amiably than was his wont he agreed
with the Squire's suggestions for the day's work.
There was to be a walk, it seemed, round the Home
Farm, and afterwards the visitors were to be introduced to the chief institutions of the village. Maggie
was to accompany the party as a matter of course.
There had been a slight fall of snow, and it needed
all the anticipations derivable from her presence to
overcome the Poet's natural dislike to encountering
it with thin patent-leather shoes. In London, and
by the fire, he liked to celebrate the praises of snow.
It required a great amount of good-nature—as of a
friendly critic—to do so afar from hansom cabs. But
something must be done to-day. Yesterday rhymes
had either held aloof, or been absolutely idiotic. He
had even become aware that the useful custom of
fitting your sense to your rhyme, or, oftener perhaps,
abandoning the former entirely in favour of the latter
might be overdone.

Mr. Jones had resumed his knickerbockers, and
though stiff from his exertions of yesterday, declined

to be left behind. Maggie laughed at the laborious way in which he crawled over the first stile they came to, and the Poet could not avoid seeing that the two were on excellent terms. It was certainly not intentionally that he diverted her attention from his rival into another and more amusing channel. Crossing a paddock not far from the house, the party came on a little herd of yearling cattle, amongst which was a young bull, who made himself very absurd by antics which would perhaps have threatened danger had he been full-grown. He attached himself instinctively to the Poet as the one who would be easiest frightened, and so greatly intimidated that gentleman that, after several futile attempts to evade the unwelcome attention, he fairly turned tail and started off at a run. This excited his enemy, as a policeman is moved to pursuit by seeing any one run away, and in spite of the reassuring shouts of the Squire—which he may have taken for incentives to speed—the Poet was soon in full flight, with the whole of the little herd capering and dancing in delight at his heels. The sight of the fugitive, his long, thin legs stretched to their utmost length, his long locks floating behind him in the breeze, was more than the gravity of those left behind could resist. The Squire roared like any full-grown bull of

Bashan, Maggie's enjoyment was as evident if less loud, and even Mr. Jones saw no reason for restraining his mirth. When they rejoined Mr. Corthee—after the next stile—the Squire did his best to conceal his merriment.

"You needn't have run," he said; "did not you hear me calling to you to stop? They're only calves. Now I want you to use your eyes here. You've heard of the 'working-man'? Oh, poetically you can make nothing of him. But you might have made something of a smock. Ever see a smock? The 'working-man' now is a fraud. He has been taken up politically and spoilt. There's as much poetry to be got out of him now as out of—my hat. There's no poetry now in agriculture. Bare as a modern stubble. Goldsmith and 'Sweet Auburn' was all very well; but now that 'a bold peasantry,' or 'a small holder,' or whatever he may have meant has died out, it seems to me absurd to try and restore him. Such things must be left to supply and demand. You might as well stick up scarecrows about the place, and call them 'a bold peasantry,' as try to make 'small holdings' prosper by Act of Parliament. Here's a bit of good land here. Do you know good land when you see it? I thought not. Well, the County Council or somebody takes a fancy to just this bit to set up a bold peasant with. Is there any sense in that? In a few years the bold peasant will be in difficulties, and I—Maggie rather—may get the land back again. And the experiment will have been rather a costly one. But the day is yet far off when the country—that means the people who talk—will be tired of trying costly experiments with other people's money—which usually means mine."

The Poet appeared to be paying no attention to the harangue, being engaged in mopping his face, which necessary operation he was aware was yet, for a poet of the modern genus, an absurd one. He glanced uncomfortably at Maggie, whose face was turned away. There was a convulsive twitching of her shoulders which showed that she was still laughing inwardly. The Squire smothered his laughter, and as soon as possible prepared to take up his parable again.

"It appears," thought Mr. Corthee—as he heard the preliminary clearing of the Squire's throat— "that I have come down here to be talked to."

"Papa," put in Maggie, "here is old Jarvis with the sheep. Surely there is poetry in old Jarvis. At all events he is not commonplace, though he has given up his smock. He says there are none to be had now."

Mr. Jones and Mr. Corthee raised their eyes and saw approaching across the grass field a very old man, clad in a suit of dilapidated corduroys, an old billycock hat, and high leather gaiters. In his hand was a sheep crook, and he was followed by a flock of sheep closely as the Poet had been followed by the calves, but in a different spirit. In rear of the flock walked, tail on ground and with watchful eye, an old black-and-tan sheep dog. As the old man came up to the party he pulled his forelock by way of salute, with a special nod in Maggie's direction, and stood still in mute contemplation of the two strangers.

"A vine day, Squire, if it udn't snow," he said at last. "You're getten some new varmers, I reckon. What 'ud the gennelmen think of my vlock now? I'm proud of my vlock, I am. Hast a ever seen a better?" raising his eyes to the Poet, at whose shoes he gave a passing glance of wonder. "You're no ways shod for varming, leastways in winter," he said sympathetically. "Happen you'll catch your death."

"He wants to know," explained the Squire, "what you think of his sheep. These gentlemen"— turning to the shepherd—"are not farmers" ("I knowed it," put in the shepherd), "they have come down from London to look about them. Perhaps, if they like it well enough, they will take the Home Farm off our hands."

"Like enough," said Mr. Jarvis sarcastically. "Lunnon! They comes from Lunnon, does they! I've heerd tell of Lunnon. Does the Lunnon people know a sheep when they sees one, I wonder?"

"We are not quite so silly as you fancy," said Mr. Jones; "we eat plenty of mutton, and ought to know a sheep by sight well enough."

"What un sort of sheep be theesen?" asked the shepherd.

Mr. Jones made no answer, and the Poet had turned his back on the discussion.

"They bin ewes, they bin," said Mr. Jarvis, after the manner of Her Majesty's Inspector of Schools when trying to find out if a little boy knows anything at all; "and now can eether ef you gennelmen tell what a ewe bin?"

Mr. Jones's face wore the pleased look of a medical student when the examiners have chanced on his *spécialité;* but before he could answer the Poet turned sharply round.

"I suppose," he said briskly, "every one knows that an ewe is a lamb."

"Haw, haw, mister, you do make me laugh, you do," said the shepherd, preparing to pass on with his flock. "I could see as you knowed summat. You learns everything up in Lunnon."

The Squire began a loud roar, which he rather awkwardly cut short in the middle. "The little ewe lamb of the Bible," he thought to himself. "Good-morning, Jarvis," he said aloud.

Maggie was in a state of perplexity. It was bad manners no doubt to laugh at the ignorance of her guests, but restraining was painful, if not absolutely dangerous. The drollest thing was that the Poet was unconscious of any slip. Probably he imagined country-folk were in the habit of bursting out laughing for very little or nothing. What was to be done with these people? Just then her eye caught a glimpse of the red brick of the old village school through the hedgerows. A path close by where they were standing led to it across two or three fields.

"Oh, papa," she said, "could we go by the school? I should like to go in for a minute. Perhaps"—turning to, Mr. Corthee—"you would come in too. I dare say schools are more in your way than old Jarvis and his sheep."

The Poet magnanimously assented.

"I thought you would have liked old Jarvis," said the Squire, rather unwisely returning to the very matter Maggie had been anxious to shelve. " I could not have shown you anything I fancied you would enjoy more. He is a walking eclogue, straight out of Virgil; though we have improved the breed of sheep, I trust, since those days. I thought he would have given you quite a pastoral feeling—Melibœus and all that. But I suppose it is cold for that sort of thing. Well, I hope you'll find something to interest you in the school. It is not my fault if you don't. You can't expect anything very new down here, and old things you don't seem to care for. Our school is about as old-fashioned as Jarvis. The kind of place Noah's grandchildren went to after the Flood. Goldsmith would have liked it; but then you don't care about Goldsmith. Dear me! dear me! Here we are, gentlemen "—with the air of a showman—" walk in."

The Poet lost no time in entering a place where at least he would be able to stand on dry boards, and be safe for a time from the intrusion of snow into his shoes. Maggie entered with him. The Squire button-holed Mr. Jones for a minute outside.

CHAPTER XIII.

THE YOUNG SCHOOL-MASTER.

"This free education," quoth the Squire to the guest, whom he detained after the fashion of the Ancient Mariner, "is a swindle. True, the working-man is let off his pence, but farmers throughout the country are still assessed to School-boards on their rentals, and it is their money which in reality defrays the cost of education in the country. It is, I suppose, a grand joke to make the farmer pay the expenses of an Act which has taken away his plough-boys, and made it almost impossible for any farm labourer hereafter to be trained, as he should be, from a youth up. I'll tell you what it is, Mr. Jones. The farmer—like the landlord—has no friends; everything is piled on him, and no one seems to see, or to care when he does see, that the agricultural industry is being ruined. Here we are now going in for over-educating everybody, and the craze has but commenced. County Councils are bitten with the same fad. The fact is the rates are being utilized wholesale with the hope of getting votes, and when we've spent the money *we may whistle for the votes.* This educating people! Look what it has done with the memories of the working-classes, and of other classes too. Why it has simply destroyed them. There's old Jarvis—never learnt to read or write, yet he could tell you everything that happened here since he was a boy, and the day and year it happened in. You'll find very few young people who, without looking at their notes, could tell you what happened last week. Now you poets, I know you must be hard up for material, but you won't get much out of modern agricultural life—what little there was the education craze has settled. In Wordsworth's day it was different, but now you might as well write poetry on a lot of plates in a plate-rack—very ordinary plates, and exactly alike. But come along inside."

The school was a Liliputian affair, without any of the splendour which causes a modern Board School to far surpass Eton or Rugby; and indeed Her Majesty's Inspector was constantly threatening to withdraw the grant if it was not at once beautified and enlarged. As the Squire and Mr. Jones entered they found that

the Poet had already betaken himself to the hot-
water pipes which ran round the school-room, and
was trying to dry, or at all events to warm, his feet.
Maggie was speaking to the master, who now signed
to the children to stand up by way of greeting the
new-comers. The Poet, who was chiefly interested
in the state of his socks, was standing with his face
close to the wall. The Critic's observant eye noticed
a glance cast on him by the master as he entered, by
which he was at first slightly puzzled. The master
was an exceedingly handsome young man, slight,
rather delicate and fragile-looking, with fair curly
hair and keen intelligent eyes. It was impossible to
see him in this little village school without thinking
that he had missed his vocation—unless that vocation
chanced to be the cutting of blocks with a razor—
and hoping that he would one day find it. The
Squire walked up and introduced Mr. Jones, who,
being good-natured and fond of patronizing, at
once entered into conversation. The work was dull
and monotonous he—Mr. Jones—feared. He was
astonished to find in such a position one evidently
intended for something higher. So he would have
gone on, glad to please when he could do so without
any trouble to himself, when a look on the young
master's face caused him speedily to veer round.

"But no doubt," he continued smoothly, "the work has its compensations. There must, even here, be some measure of appreciation," and he glanced with some cruelty and more impertinence in Maggie's direction. The meaning of the look the young master had given him as he entered the school had that instant flashed across his mind. People who fancy themselves, or who wish to be in love, may have something of the power of insight supposed to be monopolized by lovers. Jealousy—or something as much akin to it as his new-born feeling for Maggie was to real love—enabled him to discover that the young school-master was jealous.

Mr. Collins—by this name the Squire had introduced him—blushed slightly, as if offended. He had one of those tell-tale faces on which every thought is immediately advertised.

" I have nothing to complain of in that way," he said ; " in fact, a good many things to be grateful for. The interest that everybody now-a-days takes in educational matters is, or perhaps ought to be, one of them."

" I have touched him," thought Mr. Jones. " Poor fellow, I had no wish to hurt him."

As he was searching for some remark which should be at least innocuous, he found that the Poet, having dried his shoes, was approaching them. Mr. Collins was looking at him curiously, and with a smile so slight as to be almost unnoticeable.

"I must tell you," said the Squire politely, "that Mr. Corthee—my cousin—is a great poet. At least so I am told. I suppose you are aware "—to the Poet—"that we all learn Shakespeare now, and that these little brats—who had far better be working as ploughboys—are well up in *Romeo and Juliet.* I hope they will learn to conduct their courtships when they grow up in a less rough way than their fathers and mothers did—not that Shakespeare's people were always all that could be desired. The taste for poetry implanted by Mr. Collins in their young hearts will no doubt have the effect of sending those who do not themselves turn out poets, to your shop—when they have any money. I suppose there are poets even now who could do with a few more customers."

This was, for the Squire, a great piece of pleasantry, and he chuckled accordingly.

"I don't think that a too early introduction to the poets will have the effect you anticipate, sir," put in the young master timidly, "but quite the contrary. The reason Byron gave for not visiting Horace's Sabine farm was that the 'odes' had been flogged into him before he was old enough to appreciate them, and that he could never afterwards conquer his disgust. I suppose his childhood was spared the *Ars poetica.* Children who learn by rote that of which the sense is beyond them, are never likely to trouble themselves afterwards about the meaning. I am put here to comply with the Act and to please Her Majesty's Inspector—the latter an impossible task. I confess if I had my way I would never let any child even know the meaning of the word 'poetry,' or 'rhyme,' which is often mistaken for it."

Mr. Jones was staring at the speaker in amazement. What was the world coming to when a prig of a country school-master prated about the Sabine farm ? The Poet appeared to be slightly irritated by Mr. Collins's wish to cut off the customers jocosely promised by the Squire.

" Do you not think," he said, " that—to quote the Eton Latin grammar—such learning softens manners and robs them of their fierceness ? "

" No doubt," said the young master, less timidly and with a kindling eye. " And if it were certain that a rough peasant could not be as happy as a poet, I should never think these children could learn poetry enough. But in softening the manners, and teaching the understanding of poetry, and of what makes the poet—supposing the attempt not to be a mere waste of time—do you not also endow with a larger capacity for pain? It is Pan—as Mrs. Browning put it—making a pipe out of a reed, a poet out of a man. Besides," he added more lightly, " the Squire says that you, sir, are a poet; don't you think that there are poets enough, and can you willingly look on and see what an enormous competition is being prepared for you?"

Mr. Corthee made no reply. In truth he did not know what to say. Something in the first part of the master's little speech touched him strangely. The eye that had been so inoperative when turned on Maggie, now tried to look his interrogator through. Mr. Corthee had never felt any pain arising from the fact that he was—or called himself—a poet. He had been annoyed, no doubt, when rhymes had been more than usually elusive; but pain—what was there to feel pain about? Could it be possible that this poor school-master had more insight into what should be the feelings of a poet than he had? If so, it was no doubt time to stop this indiscriminate teaching of poetry. But he would sound him.

" I feel sure you have tried your hand; you speak so feelingly of the sufferings of the poet," he said, in a tone of banter which Mr. Collins ignored.

" Oh, I've made a fool of myself like a good many

others," he said. "One is obliged to write. If not because one feels—and God forbid that any one should write who cannot feel—yet because one has nothing else to do."

With this he bowed slightly, and turned towards his class again.

Maggie had heard all that passed. She now came up to shake hands before leaving. There was a look of pity in her eyes which the young man was careful not to see. Careful as he was he was somehow aware of it, and felt annoyed. He touched her hand lightly, bowed to the Squire and his guests, and in a moment more was alone again with his class.

But when his visitors had left him he was conscious that the sun had suddenly gone behind a cloud. Education had certainly brought with it, in his case, a capacity for pain. To be able to enjoy what you have no chance of acquiring is indeed a very doubtful blessing, and—"the blind boy" notwithstanding—destructive of our peace of mind. There are people, no doubt, who would be better without feelings; plenty of people, too, who are as much without them as it is to be hoped is the case with molluscs. Even feelings can be put to sleep or ignored. They wake up, no doubt, like babies, just when they are not wanted to, and then the sooner they are put to bed again the better. But he would not put his away at once. Those men, who were they, and what did they want here? But their errand did not matter to him. Pity! He certainly did not want her pity. Let her keep it for the two strangers. A poet indeed! The long-legged man was no poet. And yet he might be; and, at all events, no one could ever hope to be a true poet who had unkind or jealous thoughts of others. The long-legged man should be a poet if he wished, and if Miss Ellis wished. And the red-legged man? The red-legged man was no fool. He was clever enough to understand that look which indeed he had not understood himself. He— the school-master, who it appeared stood in need of a lesson—had better be off from here. Yet could he go? And where to go to? But this dreaming! Bah!

"Now, boys, attention. Smith—read on, please."

"''Ere rests 'is 'ed upon the lap of *h*earth.'"

"Not '*h*earth.' Smith, do be more careful with your h's."

"'A youth to fortune and to fame unknown.'"

"What do you mean by fame? Can any boy tell me what is meant by fame? Tomkins, you are holding your hand up?"

" It means being talked about, sir."

" Sometimes it does, Tomkins. Mind you don't get talked about. Now, Smith, go on, please."

> " 'Fair science frowned not on his humble birth,
> And melancholy marked him for her own.' "

" Jenkins, what do you understand by melancholy ? Do you ever feel melancholy ? "

" Please, sir, yes."

" Well, Jenkins, when do you feel melancholy ? "

" Please, sir, when I ain't had no dinner."

" Quite right, Jenkins; enough to make any one melancholy. Only you shouldn't say ' ain't had no dinner.' Don't you know that two negatives make an affirmative ? And I suppose when you've had a good dinner you're as happy as a king ? "

" Please, sir, yes."

" I don't think there is much wrong with my boys yet," thought the school-master.

148

CHAPTER XIV.

THE RECTOR'S GLASS-HOUSE.

THE parson went to bed in a joyful mood on the
night after dining with the Squire, delighted to have
come off with such flying colours in his contest with
the two impostors—as he considered them. Nor
was he in the least impressed by the mild curtain-
lecture administered by Mrs. Butler. The good lady,
who knew little about poetry, and would never have
been able to understand why a modern poet should
not be as much better than an ancient one as a new
lamp is superior—in the ideas of a practical house-
wife — to an old one, was shocked at what she
considered the rude behaviour of her good man.
A stranger was to her a blessed boon, which it was
almost impious to slight, or to accept in any but
a most thankful and humble spirit. She was glad
of a change, although she would never have dreamt
of letting her husband see that she had any aspir-

ations beyond clothing clubs; nor had she ever been
able to overcome a feeling of awe at encountering
any one who came from the great world of which
she would have liked to know a little more. But,
though at night the parson laughed off his wife's
meek disapprobation, when the matter recurred to
his mind in the morning, he owned, to himself—he
was too wise to own it to any one else—that he had
been a little brusque in his behaviour. By the time
he had breakfasted he had pleaded guilty—before
the same judge—to having been rude. Now the
knowledge of having been rude to the most humble
of his own parishioners would have come on him as
a shock and a disgrace. How much more inexcusable was it to have been rude to a stranger whom
he might never see again, and who would not have
the countless opportunities of a neighbour—and dependent—for making the return of which rudeness
is more secure than kindness. From acknowledg-
ing that he had been rude to feeling a wish to
make the *amende honorable* was for a man of his
nature only a step, and he took it at once. Scarcely
had he finished breakfast before he was on his way
to the Hall, with the intention of inviting the
literary gentlemen—whom to-day he would take
at their own valuation—to visit his church. No

doubt, without apologizing in so many words, something would occur which would give him the opportunity of obliterating the unfavourable impression which the strangers had most probably formed of his temper and judgment.

His attempt at evading his parishioners having resulted in the presentation of more than the usual number of urgent "cases," it was eleven o'clock before he found himself passing the school on his way to the Hall. As he passed the door the Squire, accompanied by the rest of the party, was just emerging. The coldness with which the Poet received his advances he welcomed as the first strokes of a well-deserved penance.

" But you will see my church ? I am proud of it, and the more so that nothing in the way of 'restoration'—with the exception of 'putting in' some stained glass—has been permitted in my time. I have no doubt you are as fond of old churches as you are opposed to old poets."

These last words had been better left unsaid, since they quickly recalled the part which the parson had taken in the discussion of the previous evening. With simulated unwillingness the Poet allowed himself to be taken in tow. Perhaps there would be some more hot-water pipes. If not there would, almost certainly, be some way of paying out the parson. The Poet was one of those whose golden rule was to do to others as you were "done by"— and more of it. It would be a golden rule of life— or a silver-gilt one, at any rate—to remember that there is no one so humble as not to be able to repay with interest an insult or a slight. Even conferrers of obvious benefits do not always escape punishment, since the majority of people are rightly very particular as to the way in which they permit themselves to be benefited. Nor does the laziness of the great majority of those whom you have benefited or wronged, always secure impunity, since lazy people appear to keep a considerable store of energy in stock wherewith to pay off their grudges. The most sanctimonious and the most truly pious people—two very different things—while precluded from revenging themselves after the manner of the worldly ones, are yet found quite equal to the occasion. The practice of heaping "coals of fire" on the heads of those who offend us has come down from King David's days, and the present followers of the art have no doubt discovered that the general baldness of the pates of their victims makes the infliction more trying than of old. It follows that it is exceedingly unwise for any one who regards his own well-being or advancement to allow himself the luxury of offending. The worst of it is that people are so touchy that a man who would make no enemies should speak neither good nor evil of any one. Sitting perfectly still without opening your mouth, though some appear to enjoy it, would for the majority be a trying and monotonous *rôle.* Your very silence too and immobility would before long be made an offence. Perhaps therefore, after all, Mr. Jones's plan of praising everybody indiscriminately is the safest. Even this plan will offend the wise; but the wise are so few that they may practically be disregarded.

Now the parson was perfectly right in saying that he had allowed nothing, with the exception of the windows, to be altered in his church since his appointment to the living, though he was no doubt wrong in thinking that the *status quo* left nothing to be desired. Many years ago he had spent a good deal of money in embellishing—as he fancied—his church with stained glass. The same habit of mind that had caused him to acquiesce readily in the abrupt ending of the Squire's collection of the poets, permitted him to think that his windows—which may once on a time have been fashionable, if they could never have been ornamental—were everything

that a lover of art could desire. Even if he had not
originally considered them admirable, he was like
other human beings in that he could soon get
accustomed to and admire what had once struck
him as inartistic and absurd. " A poor thing," says
mock modesty, " but mine own ; " adding, "and not
such a very poor thing either ! "

What religious opinions Mr. Jones and Mr.
Corthee held were entirely subject to their ideas
of art—as they knew it. Worship in what they
considered an inartistic building — not that they
worshipped often anywhere—would be to them as
revolting as an ugly parson would to their minds be
ridiculous. The Poet, in particular, had certain
undeveloped ideas, which made ninety-nine out of
every hundred church windows that he had seen
obnoxious to him, and the hundredth only laudable
as a make-shift. On the parson cheerfully remark-
ing that he thought he had some windows that
would please him, the Poet felt that his enemy had
been delivered into his hand. Maggie trembled at
the censorial look which condemned her favourites
in advance and unseen. The Critic felt pleased that
he would soon have something to criticize, which he
greatly preferred to having his art exercised on
himself. It is a well-known fact that no one more

than a doctor objects to being operated on. As
the party entered the little old-fashioned building, which the deep hues of the stained glass had
left almost in darkness, Maggie and the parson were
for the first time sensible that the designer's art left
something to be desired.

"Ha!" exclaimed the Poet, in a tone of mockery,
when he had walked half-way up the nave without
remembering to remove his hat, "this is indeed
charming. May I ask what is the subject of that
window?"

On the window to which the Poet was pointing
was depicted a pale young lady in a red velvet
ball-dress, reclining on a blue couch; by her side
was a little spider-legged table, and on the table
a cut-glass decanter, three-parts full of some liquid
which matched the dress of the invalid. By the
side of the blue couch, sat up on his tail a rather
large-sized Scotch terrier. Everything but the dog
and the young lady's face were of the brightest
possible hue.

"The young lady," continued Mr. Corthee, without
waiting for an answer to his question, "looks exceedingly unwell, and, I see, has not taken her
medicine. Perhaps when she has done so she will
feel a little better. The faithful dog is evidently

anxious. Am I right in supposing that I am looking at a representation of the raising of Jairus's
daughter ? "

" You are," said the parson huffily, " though I am
sure I don't know how you guessed it."

" Perhaps not," answered the Poet, " but the fact
is I have seen it before. Not here,"—he hastened
to add in response to the parson's look of surprise—
" but it was the usual thing everywhere in the last
generation. The ' church-window-men ' were always
raising Jairus's daughter. You have seen scores of
them, Jones ? " he added, turning to his ally.

Mr. Jones was not disinclined to enjoy or even to
assist at the parson's discomfiture. He was on the
point of sarcastically assenting, when the look he
saw on Maggie's face made him pause. He remembered with a feeling of relief that he was under no
necessity of upholding the Poet's ideas on church
windows.

" Ah ! " he said weakly. " Don't you think this
is rather good ? I've seen worse you know." In
reality he had not, and it is doubtful whether any
one was grateful for the faint praise.

The Poet withered him with a contemptuous
glance, and put Jairus's daughter on one side.

" This, too," he said—with a nod towards the large

window at the east end of the church, on which
the Twelve Apostles were represented in gorgeous
raiment—"is really admirable. The white satin
cloaks edged with gold embroidery, and the breeches
of scarlet plush—evidently Bradford make—leave
nothing to be desired. But the straw hats are hardly
suitable head-gear. I am an admirer of originality,
and the first conception of the Apostles in scarlet
plush breeches and satin cloaks was no doubt highly
original. Unfortunately it has long since been worn
threadbare."

The Squire was laughing inwardly. He was not
greatly concerned to defend the windows, though he
would have objected to subscribing for new ones.
Perhaps he thought it as well that the parson should
not have everything his own way.

Maggie's face was flaming. "I don't think that is
the way to talk of a church," she said. " I think we
had better go home."

" Unless," said the Poet—pushing his advantage,
regardless of its effect on Maggie. A mean spirit
will starve its love to feed its malice—"Mr. Butler
has any more curiosities to show us. These windows
are good ; almost too good in fact. It is indeed a
gratification to have seen them."

" I have no more—curiosities, sir," said the parson

with a rueful smile. " I agree with Miss Ellis that we had better go."

Mr. Butler left the party at the church door, and Maggie put her hand on her father's arm.

" What horrid men, papa," she whispered. " I · think them perfectly hateful. I shall never like to look at those windows again."

" My dear, I don't suppose the windows are good. Only, as they'll have to last us, it is a pity to be told of their imperfections. Mr. Jones did not seem to dislike them."

" Oh yes, he did, papa. But he did not want to displease me." She added with a blush, " I am afraid he is very insincere."

The Squire laughed. " We are all that, more or less," he said. " Now, gentlemen, we must be getting towards home "—waiting for the two friends to come up—" I want my lunch. You were awfully down on poor Butler's windows "—to the Poet.

" Please let the windows be, papa," Maggie put in pettishly. ' " I am sure we ought to apologize to Mr. Corthee for venturing to show him such things." Maggie was still very angry.

Mr. Corthee smiled a superior smile. " Art is art, you know, Miss Ellis," he said.

In the drawing-room, after dinner, no other guests

being present, Mr. Jones turned the conversation to
the school and the young school-master.

" He looks above his position," he said, in allusion
to the latter, and with a sly glance towards Maggie.
" I should say from his appearance that he is thrown
away on those young bumpkins. He should go to
London, and make his way."

" Oh, he suits us very well," said the Squire,
rather vexed that it should be imagined that any
one could be too good for Beddington. " Don't you
be putting foolish ideas into his head. From what
I've heard it is a pretty hard matter to get on in
London. What would you advise him to do there ? "

" I should advise him to try poetry," rejoined the
Critic, who was feeling angry with Mr. Corthee, and
wished him to understand that his place was only
tenable during good behaviour. " To begin with, he
looks the business, which is more "—a glance here
in the direction of the Poet—" than they all do."

" Another poet ! " said the Squire, with a snort of
vexation. " I fancied you had already too many in
the trade. What does our friend here say to that ? "

Mr. Corthee put on his most supercilious air ; he
had sufficient conceit not to feel jealous of a possible
competitor.

" I think I could survive it," he said, "but it would

be hardly fair to disturb a young man who I presume has had an imperfect education (and who has," he felt inclined to add, "no encyclopædias) by promising him the reversion of the Laureateship. Mr. Jones," he rather unwisely added, "has a very quick eye for a new poet."

"I had a very quick eye for you," murmured the Critic in a soft aside—not so faintly but that Maggie caught the words.

"Please don't find any more poets just now, Mr. Jones," she said, blushing slightly. "I think, with papa, that there are enough"—with a slight smile. "Besides, Mr. Collins teaches me the organ, and until my education has progressed a little further, it would be extremely unkind of you to rob me of my teacher."

"I had no idea of that, Miss Ellis," said Mr. Jones. "I envy him his task, though as I am not fitted to take his place, I will certainly not say or do anything to deprive you of his services. I hardly know how the discussion as to his abilities arose. He is a very striking-looking young man, especially in his present position. He might be a little lost in London, but he would be good-looking anywhere."

This last was a great piece of impertinence, and Maggie felt it as such, without perhaps knowing

why.　Mr. Jones had the habit among his intimates
—into which he had now unintentionally lapsed—of
saying in his unctuous way the most impudent
things.　He really was angry that this young fellow
should be having opportunities of meeting Maggie
with which he—Mr. Jones—was never likely to be
favoured.　He could not imagine it possible to be
in Maggie's company without admiring her.　The
young school-master-organist had been in her
company a good deal, and must naturally feel a
large amount of admiration.

The Squire evidently thought the subject had
been sufficiently discussed, and a move was soon
made for the billiard-room.　Somehow every one
wanted to go to bed early.　The Squire because
he always did, the Poet because he was vexed with
Mr. Jones, and the latter gentleman because he felt
that he was making a fool of himself; and would
prefer to continue the operation in private.　When
sleep visited his eyelids he dreamt of the young
school-master, who was blowing while Maggie played
the organ.　Then he was in the "Immortals," and
next him—which was very unlikely to happen—was
sitting, rather disguised by long locks and a little
peaked beard, the same young man.　The well-
known room was tenanted by those who had been,

or were, his familiar friends, but the face of the Poet was not to be seen there.

Maggie retired when the gentlemen went off to the billiard-room. Jealous people play their game in the worst possible way, and—moved by the Critic's ill-advised remark—she found herself, almost for the first time, thinking of Mr. Collins. Well, she supposed he was good-looking. A poet too! not that at present she had any particular admiration of the genus, of which one was, at all events, enough at a time. But it was possible that there might be desirable examples of the species. Thrown away here, was he? Poor fellow! what chance— even supposing him to be a genius—had he of doing anything here? The next day but one would be her organ lesson. For the first time she felt uneasy. She wished, unconsciously, that Mr. Jones had not said that her teacher was a poet, and handsome. And yet, what could it matter to her? She could give up her lessons if on further consideration she found him so very handsome, and if he should begin inditing sonnets to her eyebrow.

162

CHAPTER XV.

THE DAWN OF AMBITION.

In the evening of the day in which the distinguished strangers had visited his school, Mr. Collins was sitting by himself—as indeed he generally did in the evenings—in the little sitting-room over the baker's shop which it had always been taken for granted that the school-master for the time being should occupy. He had been about three years at Beddington, anxiously hoping for the day when some more remunerative, or even more congenial occupation should present itself. But nothing had offered. Here, no doubt, he might stay till he was superannuated—he was not ungrateful for the small mercy —but once at Beddington and one might as well be buried alive. Nor after the first few months did he even appear to be getting on better terms with the few inhabitants with whom he had at first seemed to have something in common. His father,

the vicar of a poor country parish, had died unexpectedly, and without having made—perhaps
without having been able to make—any pecuniary
provision for his only son, to whom, however, he
had bequeathed his own literary tastes, and the
gentlemanly feelings that are almost the only things
out of which, in these days, one can never make
any money, since the attempt causes them speedily
to vanish. He had been thankful for the offer of the
little school—indeed he had not the experience required for a more important appointment—and there
he had striven to the best of his ability to qualify himself for something higher. He had had some knowledge of music, and—for want of a better—he one
day was promoted to church organist. This brought
him a tiny increase to his small salary. His evenings
he spent in reading, being able to get any quantity
of books that he had never read, and some that he
had never heard of, from the Squire's neglected
library. Perhaps naturally, with these stores to
draw upon, he got by degrees to neglect all other
reading for poetry. He was aware that—pecuniarily
speaking—it would have been impossible to make
a worse investment of his time. But there was fame.

Some, who seem by nature precluded from making
money, are yet able to acquire fame, or, at any rate,

they find the pursuit of the latter the more congenial. It should also be the more hopeful, since it is the prize for which the fewest contend. It had not escaped his eyes—which, indeed, were remarkably keen ones—that the great majority acquire neither. Then, he may have thought, if I fail to win either money or fame, I shall win the happiness which knowledge must bring—knowledge and the consciousness of feeling more than the common herd. It was not long before he found that to have feelings above the common herd was productive more of misery than of happiness. Doubtless it is a misery which many—like St. Simeon Stylites on his column —have enjoyed. Perhaps the most annoying thing connected with the position is that the common herd —who are all as jolly as sandboys—never dream of lifting their eyes to notice what they would consider a most undesirable exaltation. It would be something to be credited, if not with superior happiness, yet with superior misery.

To the Squire he was the school-master, " a good little fellow," to whom his patron occasionally condescended. To the parson—this was still harder to bear—he was the organist, and the organist who did not always give satisfaction. To his boys— well, he felt sure his boys liked him. With Maggie he had never come much in contact until about three months ago, when by the Squire's wish he had consented—without any misgivings—to give her lessons on the organ. It was not long before he found the occupation a pleasing pain, to which he yielded the more unconsciously that Maggie did not seem to perceive that there was any awkwardness in the situation. There was no doubt that he had got to think the two or three hours a week in which she was alone with him in the church—for the presence of the little "blower" did not count for anything—worth all the rest of his days. He had opportunities of studying Maggie's face, to which he yielded the more readily from the knowledge that his inspection must necessarily be unobserved by its object. The course of his poetical studies had prepared him for the now unfashionable worship of woman; and he had met one—as he told himself— whom he could have appreciated without any special education. There was little that was pleasing in his life, and if the organ lessons had been taken out it would have been a barren existence indeed. Flowers that we are prohibited from gathering, grass on which we are requested not to walk, are better than no garden at all, and they are the flowers and the grass that we especially covet.

Not that Mr. Collins had ever gone so far as to
imagine whither his folly could lead him, or indeed
that it could lead to anything or anywhere. He had
scarcely got so far as to acknowledge to himself that
there was any folly. His was simply the romantic
feeling of a young man attracted by a beautiful girl,
made more beautiful than the reality by imaginary
endowments. It certainly was not love, and it
might never be love. That it could ever be successful love he would never have dared even to dream.
But this evening as he sat at his desk—his pen, in
which the ink was dry, in his hand—he was conscious
of a new feeling which a little experience would
have taught him was jealousy. Nothing is so easily
detected in another by a lover as the jealousy to
which he is himself unwittingly a martyr, and he
had been aware that Mr. Jones had given him credit
for taking unusual interest in his pupil. To have
recognized that he was jealous might have warned
him whither he was tending. Then that supercilious Poet ! The two Londoners, whatever they
might be, had the immense advantage of meeting
Maggie — Miss Ellis — on equal terms. To be a
worshipper is scarcely to be on equal terms with
one's goddess. The fear of falling into an abyss from
which he should be unable to extricate himself was

now first appearing to him as a remote possibility.
That the woman who was to him all that he
regarded as "pure womanly" appeared likely to
inspire others with the same feelings, gave him little
comfort. Yet he would have been still less pleased
to see her overlooked or despised. He had never
had any more doubts than had Paris as to the
correctness of his judgment, which he was not sorry
to see ratified by far more experienced connoisseurs.
Our admiration is apt to be unconsciously swayed by
that of others. What so many admire we take it
for granted must be admirable, and we prostrate
ourselves with faces towards the earth without first
raising our eyes to carefully inspect the goddess
whose glance after all might not have been so very
scorching. It never strikes us that the majority of
the worshippers whose example we are following
may have acted in the same way. But what—he
asked himself—did it matter to him who admired
her? If she was not fair to him he cared little for
whom she was fair. It was all very well to talk like
that, but alas! he was not poet enough yet to say
clever—or even foolish—things that he did not
feel. One day, if he ever blossomed into a real poet,
like the long thin gentleman, he might arrive at
this. At present poetry to him meant not even the

partaking of "all passions as they pass," still less
the attempt to portray passions he had never felt or
could feel. All that he had hitherto written was
the genuine outcome of his own feelings, and he
never desired to write anything else. In this way
no doubt wrote our first—poetical—parents, and the
departure from their rudimentary system is a ques-
tionable improvement. Poets now-a-days can not
only write about what they never felt, but also they
can be eloquent on things which no one else ever
felt either—or is likely to feel.

But would it be necessary—he sighed as he asked
himself the question—to give up the lessons?
Yesterday he had thought them so harmless. What
could there be wrong in them to-day? Perhaps,
though, they were more foolish than wrong. The
eating of the fruit of the tree of knowledge of good
and evil is not always an enjoyable, and still less
frequently a digestible meal. We were so happy
before our eyes were opened that we almost wish
that our blindness could have endured for more than
the brief days of puppyhood. If the lessons were to
be given up he would have to leave Beddington.
The stout, smooth-spoken man with the red legs
had suggested London. He had heard a rumour—
he was too ingenuous to imagine that the two visitors

could have had a hand in its circulation — that Messrs. Jones and Corthee were shining lights of the literary world. Would they stretch out a hand to him ? He did not think so, and he would prefer to make his way unaided. He had not the idea as to the material of which the London pavement is composed which moves so many to start light-heartedly on their travels. Rather he thought that, as had been the case with others, he would find the great city a stony-hearted step-mother. But from London at least one could return—he either forgot or was ignorant that very few do so—and there were two ways of returning. One way he would not anticipate that he would have to use, yet it was that by which most people come back. Success—like the Scotchman—seldom goes back at all. The alternative was a triumphant entry to a new and improved position. The Squire not merely patronizing, the parson appreciative. Miss—but it was time to stop this fooling. He laughed rather bitterly— he had been striding up and down his little room with flushed face and sparkling eyes. At least—to come back to common-sense—it was a comfort to know that the secret of the inspiration which had produced so many poems, some of which were not, he trusted, quite hopeless, was hidden in his own bosom.

If people only knew it, life might be made prosperous, and more than prosperous, happy, if they would but firmly decide to adhere to two simple rules. One of these is to make good resolutions, and the other to keep them. Either rule is useless if we discard the other, since if the resolutions are bad it is better not to keep them, and if they are not to be kept there is no use in making them at all. After all we can but do our best; make the best resolutions we are capable of—some of them will no doubt turn out mistaken ones—and keep them as well as we can. Unfortunately the resolutions that it will be easiest to keep are those which there was least wisdom in making.

Before he slept that night the young school-master had decided to try his fortune in London.

CHAPTER XVI.

IT was the last day of their stay, and not without regret—which neither would have admitted to the other—the two friends recognized that on the morrow they would be recommencing the dreary round of town life again. The flattery by which no one was taken in; the being lionized—only less unpleasant than being deserted for a new lion; the hard pavements; the too jocose cabmen; the stale, inexpressibly stale, dinners. To a certain extent, no doubt, Poet and Critic were aware that the journey had failed of being a success. Even the former may have recognized that a few days was too short a period in which to " take in " the country. A lamb he had discovered indeed—after considerable reflection—to be a lamb, but to diagnose a country maiden might require a little more leisure. He was already aware that these studies are not unattended by danger,

and the result of his " eye-practice " had been that he
had succumbed to charms by which he certainly had
not intended to be vanquished. He despised, he
loathed himself for his weakness, but his self-denun-
ciation had not the effect of making him strong.
He was a fool, he saw clearly ; but his folly, he
acknowledged, would in the case of a less distinguished captive have been pure wisdom. That
he, an illustrious and unwilling victim, had been
conquered was proof sufficient of the enemy's prowess.
There were few people with whom he would have
admitted that a friendship could be anything but
derogatory, but he did not foresee that he would have
to blush very greatly for Maggie. Then, if not rich
—he had seen and heard enough during his visit to
the country to be aware that she was not likely to
be a great heiress—she would at her father's death,
which was not likely to be long deferred—what a
rage the Squire would have been in—have an
income which would come in exceedingly handy.
There would be no necessity for spending it on this
mouldy old Hall, which could be well let to a brewer.
He and Maggie—HE always came first—would take
a house in Mayfair, where her appearance as hostess
would no doubt have a beneficial effect on his career.
There would be money enough, after the housekeep-

ing bills were paid, for the printing of sundry little
—but not inexpensive—books, which had hitherto,
for want of the necessary coin, been condemned to
pine in manuscript. Maggie's money would be put
to a good use. She, poor girl, would be a little
countrified at first. Perhaps she would always be a
little countrified, but at all events she would have
had her chance. In old age she would be able to
plume herself on the fact that a poet had written of
her in the days when she was young—for he would
write something on her. But these confounded
rhymes. Yet not the rhymes so much as the sense.
"How on earth,'" murmured the Poet softly to
himself, "did the little witch manage to catch
ME ?"

Breakfast was over, his host had left him, and he
was for a few minutes alone. He was standing by the
dining-room window, with a fatuous smile on his lips,
when Maggie, basket in hand, descended the steps
from the front door, and passed the window on her
way, as he easily guessed, to the garden, whither she
was wont to resort after breakfast—weather permit-
ting—for a conference with the old gardener. In the
centre of the large walled kitchen garden was an
old greenhouse, sheltered by an enormous mulberry
tree. Small events have often had immense influence

on the careers of great men. The Poet recognized this truth as he hurriedly made up his mind.

"The very place," he said, as he caressed his moustache. "I'll follow her at once and get it over. How extremely fortunate. I trust that ass Jones is not about. I have not seen the fool since breakfast. He has been, I think, rather too obviously inclined to be sweet on Maggie. Confound his impudence. It's hardly likely that she would have anything to say to such a fellow. And his red-striped knickerbockers too! She can be trusted to see the difference between chalk and cheese."

The Poet ran hastily up-stairs to cast a glance at himself in the mirror before proceeding to the interview which would be for Maggie such a momentous one. "It is one's duty, I suppose, to look one's best on these occasions," he murmured. The housemaids fled from the room in dismay on his entrance. After a few hasty touches to hair and necktie he hastened down-stairs again. He was conscious, as he snatched up his hat and made his way to the walled garden, that his heart was beating faster than usual, and he carefully noted the fact for future use. Before arriving at the large green door through which no doubt Maggie had preceded him, he looked anxiously back at the Hall, but there was no Mr. Jones or any one else in sight. So far so good. The old door opened inwardly, and he was careful not to make any unnecessary noise. When the door was about half open he took the precaution to peep stealthily round the corner. It was well that he did so. Maggie had disappeared, as he had expected, but a door on the opposite side of the garden, which was used chiefly by the gardeners, was ajar. His own movements had engendered suspicion of others, and he withdrew as much from sight as was consistent with keeping his eye on the other door. As he was on the point of advancing, the door he was watching opened a little wider, and two red objects were distinctly visible which could be nothing but the gorgeously-striped knickerbockers which encompassed the stalwart legs of Mr. McCawmee Jones. He closed the door gently, but continued to peep at short intervals through a chink in the rotten wood-work. In a few minutes he saw that the other door was also closed. The incident disgusted him, and he walked rapidly back to the house, chafing inwardly, and cursing—poetically—his folly in not having paid his visit to Beddington unattended. As he reached the front door he found that his heart was once more beating placidly in his bosom.

Mr. Jones, in entire forgetfulness of the startling

hue of his stockings, had evaded his friend after breakfast, having also decided to risk a farewell interview with Maggie. Rightly or wrongly, he too had come to the conclusion that she was necessary to his conceit, or his impudence, or whatever stood to him in the place of happiness, and he had decided to make her the offer of his hand. He, too, had tracked his *inamorata* to the walled garden, and was proceeding boldly to follow her towards the old green-house when from the doorway by which he was entering he saw a long slim figure in a white wide-awake—a head-dress which the Poet affected in the winter season—appearing at the opposite door. He closed his door stealthily, but some minutes elapsed before he could take his way back to the Hall. He leant back—his hands thrust deep into his pockets—against the garden wall, which shook with the vehemence of his emotions. When at last he got back to the house his face was redder than usual. One of the under-gardeners whom he passed on his way was heard afterwards to remark that he had met the gentleman with the red legs, " and his face were redder nor his legs. And blest if the cove wasn't nigh a-busting of hisself, a-trying not to laugh."

Not long after the departure of the two faint-hearted lovers, Maggie—in ignorance of the double

greatness which had been so nearly thrust on her—
came out of the old greenhouse, still talking to the
gardener. As she took her way back to the house
again, her face wore a slightly puzzled air. Possibly
—who can say?—she had rather expected to be
followed by one or other of her new admirers. There
may even have been occasions when such an experience had happened to her. Even when one is
relieved by the discovery that one has made an
inaccurate forecast, it is humiliating to have been
mistaken in a judgment as to one's attractiveness.
But on this occasion Maggie was not hurt at the
double desertion, and indeed it would have been
awkward to have had to entertain at once two
admirers. Which of the two she would have preferred she herself would have found it difficult to
say. Mr. Jones would certainly have been the
easiest to get rid of, but the fact was of doubtful
advantage to a lover. Mr. Jones's praise, if excessive,
was after all of the human sort which gods—and
goddesses—are said to prefer. He himself, if rather
absurd, was not without the desirable quality of
good-nature. It is, of course, an open question
whether the quack who can on occasion laugh at his
own humbug is less harmful than the one who keeps
up, even to himself, the pretence of being genuine.

But to have been subjected, in the privacy of the old
greenhouse, to the scorching ordeal of the Poet's
eye—which in a mixed company had been an ineffectual terror—would have been found decidedly
disturbing. Maggie's slightly puzzled air yielded
gradually to a look of content caused by a conviction
that everything was for the best in this best of all
possible worlds. She was satisfied to have been
spared a homage—or homages—to the offering of
which she might yet not have objected. Did it
follow, she asked herself, that she had therefore to
give up her ideas as to the future? She had a
determination not to grow up like a vegetable in the
bucolic fashion of which she saw so many examples
around her. She would not, if she could help it, settle
down into a country bumpkiness. Yet "bumpkin"
was unfair. Young Lovibond was no bumpkin. At
least he was not what was considered a bumpkin in
the country. He was probably wise in occupying
himself with matters which he felt capable of understanding. Maggie knew perfectly well that Mr.
Lovibond wished—for reasons which she understood
perfectly—to marry her, and he might perhaps be
able to work himself up into passion which should
be as genuine as that of any other country young
man. Affairs of the heart about Beddington were

arranged, or arranged themselves, in a rather placid
and bovine way. In London she supposed it was
different. The behaviour of the two Londoners was
probably not a fair sample of the whole, or perhaps
when these great people went into the country they
tried to do as the country people did. If so they
failed signally. A picture of Mr. Jones on his knees
in his knickerbockers on the sharp gravel, while
Mr. Corthce carefully spread a handkerchief before
kneeling on the other side, came into her mind,
and if she had had the pen of Cruikshank
she might have immortalized the imaginary scene.
Yet perhaps there are few women who would be
capable of caricaturing the most sacred of their feelings. At the bottom of her heart was a feeling of
disappointment. When the Londoners had been on
their way she had felt, " Now we shall see something."
She had indeed seen something, but doubted whether
it was worth seeing. Everything they said or did
was unreal, and she had a feeling that they wished
this fact to be evident. If the sham surface concealed anything, its presentation was an impertinence,
while if it concealed nothing it was even less satis-
factory. " Rather than have such a lover as either
of them," she was thinking, " I would put up
with Tom Lovibond."

By three o'clock in the afternoon the two visitors were seated in the train on their way back to London. The Poet had regained the state of simulated indifference which he thought becoming to the occasion. No doubt there are occasions when it is necessary to assume something. The Critic watched him not entirely without envy. He was conscious himself of feeling less smooth and perhaps a little less happy than usual. He sat with his back to the engine, and looked with a sigh of regret on the wintry landscape they were so speedily leaving behind them. There was little in the view which those who fancied they knew him would have expected him to mourn for. Dark woods, like ink-stains on a map, patches of half-melted snow on the half-ploughed fallows, swollen streams, here and there the chimneys of some old-fashioned mansion like Beddington. And in the mansion! A hospitable old squire, who could tell? And a daughter? a daughter perhaps in some way resembling Maggie. Not that it was likely that there would be many to resemble her. No, there was only one Maggie, and he was leaving her to go back to London with its shams and its smooth sayings, and its mutual and not too profitable admiration. Well, it was fate. Perhaps he had been mistaken in thinking that, for a permanence, he could endure anything else; but if that was the case it only made him out the greater fool. Quickly he thought over the incidents of what he felt had been an eventful visit; the hunting, of which he felt rather proud; the reading, which had hardly been a success; the young school-master so genuine and unaffected. It was not long before he found himself recalling his—this morning's—visit to the kitchen garden. He saw, as if he were an amused spectator, the two doors opening and the appearance at either of the white hat and the red knickerbockers. He glanced down, with a smile on his good-natured face, at his legs. His lips opened as if to address his companion. But the Poet was fast asleep.

CHAPTER XVII.

MAGGIE MAKES A DISCOVERY.

"I AM in a great rage," said the Squire at breakfast one morning, about six weeks after the visit which was concluded in the last chapter. "That young school-master has sent in his resignation. There is no such thing as gratitude now-a-days. I thought he would have lived and died here. What more could he possibly want, I should like to know? It is all those poetry fellows of yours."—"Of mine!" thought Maggie.—"They turned his head. I suppose he will go to London to starve, as so many have done before him. Confounded young puppy!" and he held out his hand for his tea-cup, with what, for the Squire, was a near approach to a scowl.

Maggie had been looking quieter for the last few weeks, as if something had occurred that required thought. She had not raised her eyes during her father's speech. She was smiling now at the vehemence to which she was so well accustomed, and which she knew, in cases of this sort, meant so little, or rather it meant a good deal—that the Squire had taken an interest in Mr. Collins, and was hurt that he was leaving. Now she had to look up, and to make some sort of answer.

"I don't think," she said, "that you are quite fair, papa. Surely Mr. Collins was not under an obligation to stay here all his life without any hope of advancement. It was very poor kindness to help him, if he was never to be allowed to help himself afterwards. You would not really wish him to stay here always. He seems to me fit for something better than a village school-master."

"Just so, Maggie. That's the way every one talks now. Above 'the position to which it has pleased,' etc.,—as we used to say. Why the deuce, I should like to know, is every one to be educated above his position in life? Of course, I wish the young fellow no ill; but what are we to do for a master? Then there are your organ lessons. Just as you were getting on so well. The next chap will know nothing about the organ. Twenty pounds for an organist; and where to get one I can't tell."

"Papa," said Maggie, blushing slightly, "did not

you know that I gave up my organ lessons quite a
month ago,"—the Squire looked up quickly from
his paper,—" when I had that cold ?"

"You hussy," said her father; "you never said a
word to me about it." Maggie looked demurer than
ever. "By the bye, I quite forgot" — with an
assumption of having remembered the fact quite
suddenly—"to tell you that young Lovibond is
coming over to see me to-day. Indeed, I asked him
to lunch."

The Squire was now looking at his daughter with
the expression seen on a dog's face when he has
done something he is ashamed of. But Maggie did
not raise her eyes.

"Very well, papa, I'll remember," was all she
said.

The Squire was not much given to "taking notice"
—as the old nurses used to say—or he would have
seen Maggie's fingers tremble as she passed him his
cup. She made an early excuse to get out of the
room. The Squire looked after her wistfully.
"Wonder how 'twill answer," he said to himself.
"He is a good young fellow. I don't see how she
could do better. It would be nice for me if she
married some one I could get on with." Yet he
did not feel quite comfortable. Maggie had never

appeared to look on Tom Lovibond in the light of a lover, but there was no one else in the field. No doubt she would allow herself to be moved by his evident wish to see her safely settled near him. The thought made him feel sadly ashamed of himself. He had approached the matter once or twice without quite arriving at it; Maggie, indeed, had not allowed him to arrive at it. Yet he knew that she understood his wishes. He felt at this moment that he had far rather have a son-in-law he could not get on with than that Maggie's inclination should be forced. Perhaps he had better explain himself. He went to the door, opened it, and called, " Maggie." No one answered. " Maggie," again. Still no answer. Perhaps he took this for a good omen; if so, he decided not to call out again. He did not see anything more of Maggie till lunch-time, punctually with which meal Mr. Lovibond made his appearance. Never before probably in that old house had a more constrained party sat down to a meal. There was Tom Lovibond—usually so blunt and jovial—blushing like a great boy, as indeed he was. A sudden change—for which he had no one to blame but himself—had come over his cousinly relations with Maggie. The three people who used to be so open-hearted now seemed each to be oppressed by the burden of a secret, and to have no longer anything in common. Not that a maiden can be always expected to wear her heart on her sleeve. But the Squire! The way in which he shuffled out of the room directly lunch was over—pretending (he who so hated pretences) that a letter he had expected to find in the left-hand pocket of his coat had been left up-stairs—was something quite new. When he was gone not a word was exchanged while the servants were clearing away the *débris.* Maggie looked at her guest as if she wished he would go. And he returned her look with another which meant that he really would oblige her if it was in his power. He knew that he was doing, or going to do, what Maggie—whatever answer she might make—would prefer that he should leave undone. He hated to vex her, but he was in love—or he supposed so. A young man who has got to suppose that he is in love can scarcely be expected to show any regard for other people's feelings. For years he had been on terms of close friendship with Maggie. They had met out hunting, and at Beddington; she had always been his beau-ideal of a "jolly girl," and up to the present time there had never been the slightest awkwardness between them. This bothering love upsets everything. In reality, young Mr. Lovibond was in love with the Squire. The Squire, he knew, wished him to marry Maggie, and he would do a good deal to oblige the Squire. Besides, it was almost necessary, if Maggie and he were to continue friends, that he should marry her. Some one else would certainly do so if he did not, and he could not afford to lose such a friend. He had not any doubt in his mind that Maggie had a sincere liking for him, but whether that was enough he could not say. Girls are so silly, and go into fits about it. Yet he mentally made an exception in Maggie's favour; there was no nonsense about her. Maggie and he would run well—in this horribly unromantic way did he put it to himself—in double harness.

"Maggie," he said, addressing her suddenly, as soon as they were alone, "will you come into the garden?"

Into Maggie's head at once popped the words—

"Come into the garden, Maud;"

but Tom Lovibond's matter-of-fact way was not suggestive, except by contrast, of the late Laureate. She smiled. One better versed than her companion in affairs of the heart would have recognized an enemy in the smile. Mr. Lovibond recognized nothing of

the sort; he had never yet found cause to dread
Maggie's smiles, which indeed—being of opinion
that one smile is very like another—he had never
taken the trouble to analyze. Maggie quickly got
her hat and gloves, and they went out together. It
was one of those fine spring mornings, pleasant but
delusive, which are sometimes seen in March, which
month often now delights to puzzle us by coming in
like a lamb and going out like a lion.

"Which way?" he inquired, as they descended the
steps from the hall door. "Shall we go to the greenhouse?"—"a comfortable place," he was thinking;
"and perhaps Maggie would not object to a pipe."
In fact Maggie had been turning towards it almost
as a matter of course, but now something made her
hesitate. She was fond of the place, and would not
carry away from it what she foresaw might very
likely be an unpleasant memory. "We will go to
the elm walk," she said; and turned in another
direction up a path which led through some shrub-
beries to the summit of a slight hill, along the crest
of which ran a row of old elm-trees. Here a gravel
walk had been made once upon a time, and there
was a rustic seat or two often used in summer. It
was one of those mornings when spring's approach
is felt by everything—bird, beast, man, and worm!

The sun shone through the bare boughs of the old
trees and made the mossy trunks gleam like burnished
copper. A lark rose from the grass in the hollow
below; the rabbits scuttled hither and thither.
Not a bad day for a young couple who loved each
other to come to an understanding. Perhaps it was
not Tom Lovibond's fault that his head was not
fully occupied—as it doubtless ought to have been—
with the affair of the heart which he nevertheless
intended to bring to a conclusion. He was well
aware no doubt that the best way, the only way to
insure success, is to take one thing at a time. Artists
who perform on several instruments at once are
seldom masters of any one in particular. His excuse
must be that Maggie had always been so identified
with his hunting that his love for her was almost a
love of hunting—and *vice versâ*. And this was the
way in which he thought fit to begin his love-making
—as he no doubt considered it.

"No more hunting, Maggie,"—then certainly he
sighed like a furnace,—"but what a famous season
we've had. Never saw you go so well. I say,"—he
continued with a chuckle,—"do you remember the
day those two fellows who were staying with you
were out? The one done up in furs in the pony
trap, and the chap who got the spill in the governor's

old pink. I twigged the old pink directly. I say, that was a good thing. What's become of them? What a game the parson had with them that evening. I thought I should have died. I believe those fellows were tremendously smitten with somebody." Maggie bit her lip, and stamped her little foot ever so gently. She did not want him to say anything, but if it was coming—if it had to come—the sooner it was over the better.

Tom Lovibond looked crestfallen. He made a note of the fact that "proposing"—or trying to propose—differed from hunting in that the latter seldom brought him face to face with a leap he wished to shirk. For the first time he doubted whether Maggie would follow his lead. He thought ruefully of a day when he might be no longer acting as pilot, but taking a line by himself. If that day came, hunting would have lost its chief charm. To prevent this was worth an effort.

"Maggie," he said, "you don't care about any one; I mean"—he was already quite red in the face, and felt, as he would have said, that he was muffing it awfully. "Maggie, would you marry me? We should be awfully jolly together. I've liked you ever since you had your first pony. I taught you to ride, and it would not be quite right for you to be piloted by any one else. Wait a moment,"—for Maggie was going to speak,—"it would please your father if you'd take me. I'd do anything to please the old man, and, Maggie, I love you, I do indeed, and we should get on famously together, I feel sure. Say you'll have me."

If not very lover-like, the little speech was manly and genuine, but Maggie could not help smiling at the conclusion. "Say you'll have it," was the invariable formula used by the cattle-dealers about Beddington—and indeed elsewhere. When they were trying to persuade a customer to buy a lot of cattle they would follow him all about the town, far away from the market, repeating, parrot-like, the not particularly enticing formula. When the fugitive came out of the shop in which he had taken shelter, there was the obliging dealer still waiting for him with his hand out. "Say you'll have 'em"—imploringly. Mr. Lovibond saw Maggie laugh, and he laughed too; he did not know why.

"It's awfully absurd, I dare say," he said good-humouredly; "no doubt I put it badly. But that's of no consequence"—that was all he knew about it. "May I tell your father we are going to make a match of it?"

Now Maggie had a strong feeling of friendship for

her companion, and, never having been really in love, might have fancied that it would be possible to get on well enough without anything more ardent. Her father's wishes would have come, too, almost as a command—for the reason that he never commanded. There might have been occasions when she would have accepted her present suitor almost gladly, but, for some reason or other, the present was not one of them. It would be absurd of course to suppose that the news she had just heard of the young schoolmaster's resignation could have had any effect on her feelings. Yet perhaps it would be more absurd to lay down strict rules as to what shall move, or not, the feelings of a young woman. The young schoolmaster was nothing to Maggie, yet she was in some way disturbed as she let her thoughts wander on what might be his career. Would he have a career? Mr. Jones had prophesied that he would; but how did Mr. Jones know? Now young Lovibond would never have " a career." Any girl who married him might make up her mind at once to that. She knew no one who wished less for a career, or to whom—if thrust on him—it would be a greater bore. He would lead a useful life, no doubt. And he might be trusted to " put in " a fair amount of hunting. Why—she thought—should not Tom and I stay as we are. There is no necessity for any change. Papa won't mind if I don't marry any one else, and Tom would never be so silly as to mind.

"Tom," she said, and there was a tear in her eye —she was disappointed, so she put it, in him for being after all as selfish as other people. But here she wronged Tom, who was not sufficiently in love to be really selfish. There is no selfishness like that of your true lover—"would it not be better to keep friends. We are not lovers, are we?"—("I am," dissented Tom)—"and there is no use in making believe. I don't feel that I love you. Indeed, I don't love anybody—in that way—and I don't feel that I ever shall."—They all say this, and how comforting it is too.—"Let us stay as we are. It will be much jollier. Papa will be just as glad, if you are not offended; and you won't be offended, will you? We will tell papa we are not going to make geese of ourselves."

Naturally Mr. Lovibond looked rather taken aback. It is a question whether, even when one wishes a woman to refuse one—which was not Tom's case— it is possible to escape a slight feeling of not very permanent annoyance at one's wish being granted. But then he had plenty of common-sense.

"Well, Maggie," he said sheepishly, yet not without an inward consciousness of relief. "It must be just as you like. Of course I could not bear not to be friends with you, and, if you won't do the other thing, the friendship is a good deal better than nothing. There isn't any one else, is there? Perhaps one day you'll think better of it. I'm like you. Most likely I shall never care for anybody—except you, of course," he added as an afterthought, and by way of tribute to the occasion. "Now we'll tell the governor that we are sorry to have to disappoint him. I say, Maggie"—another afterthought; he may have fancied a refused man no less than an accepted lover had certain rights—"I must have a kiss, you know. Just by way of letting one down easy, you know."

He was approaching awkwardly, when Maggie, with a frown and heightened colour, moved quickly away. "Don't be silly, Tom," she said. "That would spoil it all. Now, if we've said all there is to be said on the matter, we will go back to the house again."

So they walked back to the house, Maggie keeping about a yard in front and looking over her shoulder occasionally. Her lover's final proposition—if, indeed, he was her lover—had suddenly made it quite clear to her that she was not the least little bit in love with him.

CHAPTER XVIII.

WE may know people, as we think, intimately for a number of years, and yet have a very incorrect idea as to how any particular event will move them. This is the less strange, as we are frequently astonished at the totally unexpected effect on ourselves of events for which we had imagined we were thoroughly prepared. An introduction to some wild animals from foreign lands may even determine a countryman—who has never been fifty miles from home—to travel. The strange beasts were very likely ugly, and a sight of them might have been expected to be deterrent. Could it have been the sight of the two strange and, as he thought, outlandish beings which had struck a spark of discontent? If so, it was certainly no wish to resemble them which had determined the young school-master to start on his travels. The desire of seeing the world had but lain dormant, and a thrust from any stick would have awakened it. At any rate, as the Squire had said, he had made up his mind. He spent many nights looking over his manuscripts. Many of these he burnt; of the remainder he was sometimes hopeful, oftener despairing, and from the last state of mind he recovered slowly. But he could do better, he told himself, when he got away from Beddington. He would go at once, before he made a fool of himself. He shivered on the bank looking at the stream which would bear him he knew not whither, but he was none the less determined to take the plunge. Sending in his resignation was casting. himself adrift, quitting the haven where the storms would never reach him, the petty port where those fine ships, *Honour* and *Glory*, never put in. Whoever would get aboard these must first cross the bar.

The Squire's anger, of which he was soon made aware, hurt him, though from a knowledge of his "patron's" character he could understand the feeling by which it was aroused. He could see, too, that he rose distinctly in the Rector's estimation, and this from one who perhaps regretted his own now irrevocable renunciation seemed to him to argue well for his intended move. The parson may even have been conscious of a little mild—surely all clerical passions except piety are, or ought to be, mild—jealousy. Here was a young man who might play his part on the stage from which he—the parson—had retired.

One evening the young school-master went up to the Hall to say good-bye. A change had come over him, and he looked, as indeed he felt, eager and self-reliant. His soul—not the soul of one who was to live and die, as the Squire thought was his duty, a humble village school-master—was in his eyes, as Maggie, in a few kind words, wished him well. They chanced to be alone, and he held her hand—she was the only fair and noble woman he knew, and he was leaving her—for a moment longer than was necessary. He could not prevent that wistful look from showing itself—the desire of the moth for the star. Audacity! perhaps. Nothing is more astonishing to the vast number whom everything astonishes, than the unexpected audacity of the most retiring and bashful people. But then it must be remembered that they have never been spendthrifts of their courage, and can draw, when occasion demands it, on their reserves.

"Give me something—some little thing by which to remember you—and Beddington," he murmured.

Bold as he was, he dared not omit the qualifying clause. Maggie looked up at him startled by something in his voice. It was impossible—or at least she found it so—to look into that hopeful, impassioned face, and those eyes which were surely a poet's, without blushing. To refuse the tiny favour by which he appeared to set such store were mere objectless cruelty. She was wearing a single white rose in her bosom, and upon this the young man's eyes were now fixed. Slowly, unwillingly—for " the gods themselves cannot recall their gifts"—she detached it from her dress, and gave it him with a hand that trembled from some new and incomprehended feeling. He took the perishable gift calmly enough, but no sooner was he alone than he kissed it rapturously. It was certainly the first time he had ever kissed a flower. Had he not been the merest novice he would have had no difficulty in discovering that Maggie was strangely disturbed. How different, she was thinking, from the day when Tom Lovibond had asked her to marry him. Here was one who would certainly never ask her to marry him. One whom she might never see again—whom perhaps she did not wish to see again. What was there in it to make her feel so happy? She was not so vain as to be pleased by a proof—for a proof it clearly was—of her power to hurt one to whom she wished well. Undoubtedly she was pleased. She smiled as she went up-stairs. She smiled at her charming face—all blushes—in the glass; at the spot where the rose no longer bloomed. The rose was gone; was anything else—she wondered—gone with it? No one—not even a Duke of Westminster—can give anything away, and yet be quite the same. Sometimes to poor givers—what a blessed inducement to charity —the gift brings wealth. So the young school-master was going, and she would see no more of him—or of the rose. She did not trouble herself to inquire what he would do with the latter, but she did not imagine that he would throw it away when faded. The rose and its new owner were both gone out of her life. And yet she did not feel as if it could be so, but was in some way conscious of a completeness hitherto unknown.

The day soon came when Charles Collins left Beddington. He must be a poor young fellow, though on the way perhaps to riches, who does not on leaving home take a backward look from the last eminence whence it is visible. Is the old home an obscure one, his eye searches out all the more carefully the spot where it stands half-hidden between more pretentious buildings. So homely, so retiring, and so dear. If the old home stands prominent and stately on the opposite hill, a place any one might be proud of, it

is of course all the easier to regret it.   Then having
taken one last look you pass on.   If it was not your
home, but only the place where you left your heart,
you look back, and back, and back, and it will almost
certainly be dark before you reach the first stage of
your journey.

CHAPTER XIX.

THE CRITIC'S THUMB.

THREE months have gone by, during which time
nothing had been heard by the inhabitants of Beddington of their old school-master. He appeared to
have suddenly passed out of their lives. At first
Maggie frequently thought of him and wondered
how he was doing. Gradually she thought of him
less and less often, until now his memory was almost
as faint as that of the rose which she could not yet
quite forget that she had given him. " The absent
are always in the wrong " in having left any one
whom they wish to retain special interest in their
movements. There is no doubt, as Solomon remarked, a time for doing everything, and for a lover
the time to leave is when he has a desire to be
forgotten. There are times no doubt when an exit
will more certainly have this effect than at others.
Notably when the young woman has suddenly

discovered, rather to her dismay perhaps, that her thoughts have been dwelling too much on one who, socially or otherwise, would be thought by her friends unfit to be so honoured. The departure of the ineligible young man brings her to what those friends would call her senses, and her pride assures her perhaps that she never thought of him; certainly that she will never think of him again, and the more frequently she has recourse to this aid the more confidently may it be asserted that she is thinking of him all the time.

On reaching London Charles Collins had taken lodgings in a quiet street leading out of the Strand. They were about as bare and uncomfortable as London lodgings generally seem to those who are not to the manner born. Knowing no one, it was not long before he pined for a friendly voice or for a sight of the country. Sometimes he would have given up both these hopes for a word of praise which should have brought him the much-needed assurance that he was not labouring in vain. If successful people only remembered how a little sympathy assists or even makes more capable those who are struggling beneath them, they would not— for it is only the impostor who trembles for his monopoly—so often pause to consider whether the word of praise is, under the circumstances, excusable. In fact, flattery is never more excusable than when its objects stand in need of a tonic which it is unlikely they will offer in their turn. To churlishly refuse is to put an insurmountable obstacle in the way of many aspirants. True that even with a little praise and sympathy few are capable of rising very high; but until the glow of a little kindness has been experienced, the majority are incapable of rising at all.

June, and here he was, high up among the chimney-pots and the smoke thereof. *Fumus et opes strepitusque.* He had indeed plenty of the first, to make up perhaps for the absence of the second. The third hardly reached his attic. The cats on the roofs did their best at night-time to incite to elegiac poetry. If their bodies had been inhabited by the souls of poets to whom the *coup de grace* had been administered by Reviews or Quarterlies, with a cruelty now happily out of date, their shrieks could scarcely have been more heartrending. They came indeed as an incitement to modern bards to wail out their souls in pessimistic discontent and anguish. Perhaps there is room for thankfulness that the temptation is sometimes resisted. What a place whence to gather inspiration! Fortunately, if the most lovely scenes cannot convert the average Cockney into a poet, the " born " poet is independent of his surroundings. To the true poet all places are equal. *The Song of the Shirt, The Bridge of Sighs,* cannot be written again—cannot even, I am happy to think, be imitated—but there will always be plenty of inspiration in London smoke—for the inspired. Yet as, in these days, poets are without "intuition," it is as well to be able to work on a *substratum* of country life. I have known a boy, thirteen years old, whose parents were wealthy, yet who had never seen a bird's-nest, or even a primrose in its native home. Should this youth take to poetry, his ideas of the country may be trusted to be at least original, and it might be predicated of them that they would appeal chiefly to those to whom "a day in the country" was an unwished-for joy.

For two months Charles Collins had been occupied in re-writing and in re-arranging his manuscripts. He then thought it was high time to look out for a publisher. Perhaps there is no task more hard for a novice than to hit on a suitable publisher. Publishers must laugh—those of them, at least, who have any sense of humour—at the manuscripts sent for their kind consideration which are often quite

out of their "line." There is very little room in the
world, but still room for a "literary agent," who
should advise the inexperienced author as to who
would be the fittest recipient of the good thing.
There are presumably publishers who would shrink
with horror from printing any ridicule, however
masked and courtly, of the G. O. M. Others who
would rather prefer that Tory principles should be
lugged in anywhere and anyhow—by the heels.
There are subtle distinctions which a novice is
incapable of arriving at, ignorance of which causes
him to lose time, temper, and postage. As the
world is ruled by "the rule of contrary," it is almost
a matter of certainty that a young author who has
no one to advise him will send his first venture to
the wrong man.

Then, too, Charles Collins was unfortunately
ignorant that poetry, except in very rare cases indeed,
is a "drug." There was no one to give him this
information, which indeed he would scarcely have
credited. To him poetry seemed—amongst so many
modern shams—almost the only genuine thing left.
Surely no one would grudge a few pence, or a few
shillings, for a peep into the unknown. He forgot
what an enormous amount of affected stuff, which
could by no stretch of meaning be called genuine,

had been published between the days of Chaucer and our own, and that genuine poetry was in danger of being swamped. *Rari nantes in gurgite vasto.* To these few survivors it scarcely appeared that it was any one's business to throw life-buoys. *The Golden Treasury* has made a laudable attempt to rescue some of these, and to assemble them in a sort of poetical Sailor's Home, from which Dibdin—properly or the reverse—is excluded. The way in which Mr. Jones and his friends talked about poetry would mislead any—with the exception of the initiated— who heard them. The majority, of course, are ignorant that there are people who live by telling other people that they are poets—and what not. One naturally gets to consider that a guild to which one awards the decorations must be a grand one, and nobody—except the very few people who are poets and have no patrons—is greatly hurt by the arrangement.

But the first glow of enthusiasm is not easily damped. If Mr. Collins had heard these sad tidings —even from the mouth of a poet who had failed— he would never have believed a word of them. Experience teaches more credibly than one sent from the dead. When he had completed the arrange- ment of his manuscripts—as one about to open a new shop is careful to show off his goods to the best advantage—he began to offer them for sale. He was modest, and did not expect a rush of customers eager to purchase, nor to be invited—within the week—to lunch at Windsor Castle. It was well that he did not allow hopefulness to expand into certainty. Any approach, even to hope, should be as far as possible discountenanced when dealing with a publisher. One day his little parcel returned from its first voyage. It was accompanied by a note, whose courtesy was the more striking as there was no visible sign to show that the manuscript had been studied in the most cursory way. The young poet took it very lightly. Indeed, he rather pitied the publisher for a mistake which would no doubt be a very costly one. " He will repent," he thought to himself, " when some one else has it." This opinion he got by slow degrees to fear was a mistaken one.

By the end of the three months the manuscript had been about a good deal, and had seen more of London than its owner. It had entered the lofty portals of limited liability companies, and had ventured also into some very modest-looking edifices, which for all practical purposes were probably not inferior to their showy rivals. To whatever class of establishment it journeyed it always came back—like a bad shilling, or the affectionate but unappreciated dog which you cannot lose.

To-day, as he is going rather slowly up the narrow staircase—his step has lost a little of its youthful buoyancy in the last few weeks—he encounters his landlady, who draws on one side to let him pass. This she has the less difficulty in doing, as she is extremely thin.　Her long, dark, anxious face is seamed with tiny wrinkles.　The ill-luck and misfortune to which she has been a life-long victim, poor soul, have given her a distaste to any one with at all a prosperous look.　Appearances are deceptive, but even so she had very few opportunities of feeding her dislike.　When chance brought Mr. Collins to her door, she imagined that for once she would have a lodger favoured by fortune, whom therefore it would be her duty to snub.　Gradually she had been changing her opinion.　Within the last week or two he had indeed looked so miserable that she had become convinced that she might take him—metaphorically—to her bosom, without being inconsistent. She had noticed the parcel carefully packed and re-packed, and knew well what it contained.　A long experience of authors had made her look with certainty for its return, and even approximately to fix a date for its delivery.　When it had returned

several times she began to feel towards her unsuccessful lodger as towards a son. Now, as he was
passing her on the stairs, she said, in a deep tragic
voice in which was yet something which was certainly not sorrow—" It has come back again." He
took no notice of a warning with which she had
probably favoured him before. Only his steps
seemed to go more slowly towards his attic, as if he
would defer the unpleasant sight. Arrived at his
room, the first thing that his eye fell upon was the
manuscript in its new wrapper—he had now quite a
number of these—lying on his table. The days were
passed when he used to feel confident that on
opening the parcel he would find inside a note or
some kindly message that would mitigate the blow
—even perhaps a line requesting him to call with
the manuscript on some future day. But even
sanguine people require some little occasional mental
" pick-me-up" if they are to remain sanguine.
Hitherto his hope had had no encouragement to feed
on. He tears open the parcel mechanically, quite
prepared to find that it had been simply re-packed,
without any one having taken the trouble to read it.
He was getting clever at discovering the slightest
signs of perusal, and could tell to a page where the
" reader" had felt an access of weariness—in the few

P

cases where he had not been weary before beginning. The manuscript on the present occasion had only left him two days. It had got apparently to be fonder of home, or to return—as to its ark—as if disgusted with what it found outside, and, unlike Noah's dove, at intervals each shorter than the previous one. The day might come—must come—when it would decline to go out at all. On the present occasion he found the usual courteous lithographed note. He looked wearily at the corner of the first page of his manuscript, where, if anywhere, some sign would be found of its having been " considered." He had several times found this first page marked with cabalistic signs and numbers, which, as he could not erase them, had necessitated re-writing. There was sign enough of "consideration" to-day, for on the right-hand bottom corner of the first page appeared a huge black thumb-mark. Fearfully he turned over the leaf, expecting to see the same sign-manual—he hoped not quite so black—on the second page. But it was not there. He could only feel a doubtful joy, since it became evident that the gentleman with the thumb had not been able to keep up his interest very long.

Recognizing that things were getting serious, he nevertheless set to work to rub out the thumb-mark.

It was some time before he found that it was not to be removed. The page had to be re-written. How he was getting to hate that first page, which he used so short a time ago to think contained his *chef-d'œuvre*. How wearisome to him now was every turn of expression on which he had so prided himself. If the reader—he thought—had only read it as often as I have, one could understand. When the page had been re-written, something led him to put the spoilt page into his desk instead of tearing it up. "That thumb," he thought, as he put the page away, "is something of a curiosity. I've heard that no two thumbs are alike, and I can certainly not expect ever to see a thumb-mark like that again."

Having selected from his list a new publisher—he was at least careful not to send his manuscript twice to the same firm—he lost no time in starting it forth again. Its return was now delayed for some ten days, at the end of which time it re-appeared, and on being opened was found to have brought back another thumb-print. This last the young author speedily compared with the first one, and, with the aid of a microscope which he had brought with him to London—and which had hitherto laid neglected, and almost forgotten, in a corner—he discovered that the two thumb-marks were identical. This puzzled

him a good bit, since he had had the idea—common
to youthful authors—that each firm of publishers
had separate "readers." This illusion he saw must
in future be discarded. Evidently the number of
publishers which he had imagined unlimited, was,
practically, much smaller. Yet the discovery was
not without its bright side. Supposing all publishers
to have but one "reader" between them, his manuscript would only have been condemned by one—
perhaps prejudiced—person, instead of by quite a
host. If, however, the man with the thumb was
ubiquitous, it was hard to see how he could be
avoided. Nor indeed was there any obvious way by
which he might be discovered and—if such a thing
were possible or allowable—propitiated. He felt
very angry, for indeed he was but human.

"Who the devil," he asked himself with a stamp
of the foot, which nearly proved too much for the
crazy flooring, "is the fellow with the thumb?"

213

CHAPTER XX.

MR. WADHAMS, of the firm of Wadhams, Skimmery and Co., publishers, etc., etc., sat in his office
one June morning, as it was his custom to sit for
an hour or two throughout the year. Mr. Wadhams
might truly have advertised himself—only he would
have done nothing so dreadful—as (in two senses)
"the oldest publisher in the city of London." Perhaps the description was rightly rejected as likely to
suggest a picture of senile decrepitude of which the
elderly head of the ancient firm was in no sense an
example. Advertising has developed into a fine art,
and while some of the well-known advertisements
which we read every day on the walls may be admirably adapted to their purpose, it would seem as
if the talented gentlemen who act as advertisers'
designers cannot always resist the temptation of a

joke at the expense of their employers. The firm who announce everywhere that they are "the largest manufacturers in the world," are probably the most gigantic victims to this love of combining sport with business, and may be presumed to be unaware of the enormous bulk with which the partners are individually credited by the public who run and read. Some of us may have been so fortunate as to come across very large manufacturers indeed. Amongst these millers and bakers—publicans can hardly be termed manufacturers, though no doubt they are so to a greater extent than is generally imagined—will have been noticed as conspicuous by their girth. Farmers were once on a time very big manufacturers, though now even in the best farming districts they are chiefly noticeable for a lean and hungry look, caused no doubt by anxiety and perpetual running to and fro. But—the largest manufacturers in the world! One cannot help wondering where and by what jury this mammoth boast was verified, and how it was possible for the competitive examinations, that must surely have been necessary before the award could be justly given, to take place without the newspapers bestowing upon the contest at least as much space as they give to a baby or a barmaid show.

Mr. Wadhams was an exceedingly handsome old gentleman, and had for a generation or two been considered one of the chief ornaments of the trade. He was still what some ladies would call "an old duck," or "a dear old thing." He had blue eyes which were still tolerably bright, a quantity of the most lovely grey hair which he wore rather long, white whiskers which met under a rather prominent chin, a frock coat with the merest shade of blue in it, a white waistcoat, and an aquiline nose. It had always been his department to be courteous and kindly to all comers, and the practice of courtesy and kindness had become—not a second nature, since that would suggest, what was certainly not the case, that he had been originally without any great share of these qualities. It was of course necessary, in a great commercial undertaking like that of Messrs. Wadhams and Skimmery, that one member of the firm should be a hard and practical business man, and it had been discovered that "our Mr. Skimmery" —Jorkins *mutato nomine*—might be trusted when necessary not to be too courteous or too kind. But there were still occasions when the head of the firm asserted himself, and the qualities for which he was known. On the day that he so asserted himself there was wrath in the bosom of "our Mr. Skimmery," and joy in the heart of at least one impecunious author, who might have been impecunious for ever if he had not luckily happed on the hour and the man.

It was old Mr. Wadham's custom—except on these special occasions—to drive up in his brougham, walk quickly through the shop or office to his private room, and there seat himself calmly at his writing-table. When he had sat there an hour or two without doing anything in particular, and very often without being interviewed, he would rise and go away. To-day he seemed to be waiting for somebody. He had been sitting at his writing-table about an hour, amusing himself by tracing his profile —of which he was justly rather proud—with a very long white forefinger, when a clerk entered to say that Mr. Jones was waiting to see him.

"Mr. McCawmee Jones?" inquired the publisher; and being answered in the affirmative, he gave orders for the Critic's admittance.

Any person who had only seen that gentleman on the rare occasions when he masqueraded in what he considered bucolic apparel, would have had considerable difficulty in recognizing him in his town clothes. Mr. Jones agreed with Charles Lamb in thinking that it was no less absurd for a landsman to go down to the seaside carrying his town necessaries than for a fisherman to go up to see London with his fishing-tackle on his back. Wherever he went he strove that his costume, at any rate, should not clash with his surroundings. Failure to harmonize with these last was owing—as in the case of his brilliant-hued knickerbockers—to too ardent a wish to shine. He was now dressed like an ordinary man about town, but somehow the "get up" did not appear to suit him any better than that which had made him look ridiculous in the country. Indeed, it would have required a far larger outlay than he could afford to provide a separate suit for each of the various intellectual and athletic contests which it was his pleasure critically to preside at with more or less of success, while it was impossible for the smartest tailor to reflect the rapidity of his chameleon-like changes. At the present moment he presented the appearance of a country grocer who had unexpectedly come into a small fortune which he was expending in seeing life in London.

"Ah, Mr. Jones," said the publisher, extending two of his long white fingers, but without rising from his chair. "How do you do, Mr. Jones? I had a little matter to speak to you about"—here the old gentleman paused to consider—"Ah! yes;

some manuscript verse by a young man unknown. Mason? Gray? I cannot remember the name."

"If it was Collins," said Mr. Jones, "I cannot recommend you to take up the book."

"I thought I was very near it," returned the publisher. "You have not been very long in making up your mind. Why, you only had the book two days ago."

"Quite long enough, Mr. Wadhams, I can assure you," replied the Critic glibly. "Besides, I had seen it before."

"Oh, indeed," said the publisher, not without interest; "at Smedley's, perhaps?"

"Yes," said the Critic coolly, "and also at Trumpington's."

Mr. Wadhams frowned. It may have struck him that the arrangements as to publishers' "readers" required revising. The effect, however, of the disclosure was different to that which the Critic expected.

"I looked into that manuscript myself," he continued, "certainly without giving a great amount of time to it, and I fancied I saw signs of—well, not genius perhaps, but more than the ordinary amount of talent. That is not saying much, you think? Our Mr. Capon"—this was the Co.—"also glanced at it, and we rather anticipated that you would have recommended our taking it in hand. Who is the writer?"

"I don't think he has written anything before," said Mr. Jones, rather surlily. He was vexed that the partners should interfere with what he considered his prerogative.

"Do you know him?" asked Mr. Wadhams, with a look intended to be a piercing one, but which glanced harmless from the pachydermatous Critic.

"I have seen him," he replied, "but, independently of any merits the manuscript might have, there are so few people who ever dream of reading poetry that to publish verse by an unknown writer means almost certain loss. There are such a vast number of minor poets already. There are fifty-two——"

"Yes, I know," said the publisher, with a smile, "and for some of them Mr. Jones is responsible." (The Critic, jocosely—"I don't want to be responsible for any more.") "But"—with a relapse into dignity—"I did not wish you to consider the question of probable profits; merely to advise us as to literary merit. Thank you, Mr. Jones;" and the publisher put out the two thin white fingers again with a view to closing the interview.

When he was alone again he sat for awhile at the

writing-table tracing his aristocratic profile—as was usual with him when thinking of anything—with his finger. When he had traced it satisfactorily for the eighth time, he had come to a conclusion.

"I do not think," he was saying to himself, "that Jones is a mean fellow. Can he possibly have a spite against this new man? He may be wise in his generation in wishing to keep down aspirants. But it would serve the same purpose to dethrone a few of his idols. Well, he does that occasionally"—with a smile. "I will look into this manuscript myself. I was certainly struck with one or two things that I chanced upon."

He felt pleased—as an octogenarian could hardly help feeling—to find himself still capable of even a little self-assertion, and walked through the shop to his brougham with quite his old air of authority, causing the clerks to look inquiringly one at the other.

Having decided to take up the matter, Mr. Wadhams directed a note to be sent next day requesting Mr. Collins to be so obliging as to forward his manuscript for re-perusal. No doubt the young poet, when he received the welcome missive, would have been greatly astonished and excited if he had had any idea how unusual it was for a publisher to re-consider a decision, which indeed, he had not always the chance of recalling. As it was, he did not allow what ought to have been his injured dignity to prevent him from feeling exceedingly pleased. To avoid delay he put the manuscript in his pocket forthwith, and hurried off to * * * Street, where he rather amused the old publisher—who happened to be on the premises—by his breathless haste. Charles Collins now enjoyed his first conversation with one of those who make the fortune—every now and then—of authors. It is astonishing how many authors never arrive at an interview which they may consider—without any just reason—the one thing wanting to their happiness. It is even possible for a man to have written a successful book, and yet to have no idea of the personality of any member of the firm which is responsible for its appearance. Even if he has once or twice been interviewed by a respectably-dressed gentleman seated at a writing-table, he has known no better than his hat whom he was talking to. Great men, no doubt, are in the habit of making themselves too common; but for little people to make themselves difficult of access is not in these days to develop into a mysterious godhead. In fact, nothing is more ridiculous than the pretence of hiding what does not exist.

Mr. Wadhams received his new client courteously, explaining that he thought it possible the firm might, on a first perusal, have overlooked the merits of his poems.   In fact the old publisher was scrutinizing the young man keenly.   It required no deep scrutiny to discover that he was thin and pale, and the coat was certainly a little—or not a little—threadbare. The eyes—what eyes they were !   Mr. Wadhams was pleased with his self-assertion, and quite prepared to acknowledge a genius whom nobody else had discovered.

"Don't misunderstand me, Mr.—Mr. Collins.   I can't promise anything.   We will let you know our decision in a few days.   But I may as well tell you —if you don't know it already—that you will never make money by poetry.   We never make any either. Why not try your hand at some prose ?   Perhaps you have tried it.   No ?   All the more reason for beginning.   New writers are every now and then original.   Send us something for our magazine.   We will try and consider it favourably, and we will let you know very shortly about the poems.   Good-day, Mr. Collins.   Glad to have seen you."

And the young author went home.   It was the first word of encouragement that he had heard since he came to London, and he had not known how much he wanted it. Write prose! Of course he would write prose. He had never written any, and considered it would be as easy as we deem everything we have not attempted. He was astonished to find himself—when seated at his desk—at a loss how to begin. True, he did not know what subject to write about. Perhaps it is a mistake to write prose or poetry without having any prejudice in favour of a subject. When he was writing poetry he had never found any difficulty in the choice. Unconsciously his hand stole to a part of his desk where were a number of unfinished poems, some of them mere sketches. Must he really give up this congenial work for prose? Harnessing Pegasus to a bread-cart with a vengeance! Would it be possible, he wondered, to turn some of these sketches into prose? At first glance it appeared little short of sacrilege; and yet—he looked at the sleeve of his coat. Its threadbare condition had not escaped his notice any more than that of Mr. Wadhams. He thrust his fingers into his waistcoat-pocket, and brought them out again with two sovereigns and some silver. When that was gone he did not know where to get any more. "Needs must," he said to himself, "when the devil drives. There are good and bad devils. Perhaps this may be a good

one ; " and he began at once to turn over his manuscripts with a view to choosing the prosiest of them
for the new experiment. As he glanced over the
papers the idea of the transformation became less
and less unpleasant. The care with which his ideas
had been thought out and compressed made it easy
to expand them. Here was one which he would
immolate—regretfully—on the new shrine. "An
old Mill." His fancy began to paint and embower it
with all sorts of poetic accessories—lichen, and what
not. It might be made, he felt sure, to look poetical
even in the most prosaic of dresses, and he would
take care that the dress was not too prosaic. Having
thus salved his conscience he set to work, expanding
and elaborating. In three days he had finished, and
no one who had not himself made the same attempt
would have guessed how it had been done. I have
pleasure in advertising this method of turning an
honest penny for the benefit of the million or so of
unappreciated bards—among whom I do not include
the fifty odd minor poets of Mr. McCawmee Jones's
manufacture, some of whom I fear are also unappreciated—who have drawers full to overflowing with
unpublished poems which cannot by any other means
be converted into the smallest coin of the realm.
They will discover with satisfaction that the practice

of their laborious and unremunerative art has at
least taught them to write " Queen's English "—as
distinguished from the slipshod inaccuracies which
are the *spécialité* of the unchastened and inarticulate
novelist.

The new plan proved a success.   In a few days a
note arrived from Messrs. Wadhams, Skimmery and
Co. accepting "An old Mill," and intimating that
the firm would undertake the publication of the
poems "on shares."   This last, though meaning but
little probable profit in the case of a new author,
was yet better than nothing.   Mr. Wadhams, while
intending to be good-natured, had nevertheless the
objection to being too generous which is felt by
many business men who are yet without the fear of
their particular Jorkins.   In a week arrived a cheque
for five guineas for the magazine article, together
with an intimation that any future paper from the
same pen would have favourable consideration.
Would it be possible — or useful—to imagine a
publisher who should do more ?

CHAPTER XXI.

A GLIMPSE OF FAME.

It is not now the fashion to relate one's dreams on coming down to breakfast in the morning. Yet the custom, if slightly vulgar, had a good deal to recommend it. It was certain to be productive of amusement, and of amusement there is not too much now-a-days. How well one remembers one's maiden aunt unfolding her budget of nightmares. The custom was also an incentive to invention, since inferior dreams required a considerable admixture of fiction if they were to compete successfully with the nightmares of those who had supped—with a view to dreaming—wisely and well. In Biblical days dreams were found exceedingly useful for the conveying of opinions or warnings, which the monitor—possibly with a view to escaping personal violence—preferred to offer in a form to which he least possible objection could be taken. It would be absurd to quarrel with opinions involuntarily evoked, and which the intended victim had the option of regarding as the wanderings of a disordered fancy or the outcome of an indigestible meal.

Charles Collins's dream on the night after the receipt of the publisher's letter and enclosure was not of a very startling description, which was of the less consequence as he had no one to whom he wished to tell it. He dreamt that he was in the old school-room at Beddington, and that Maggie came in, accompanied by two strange, outlandish-looking people, in whom—allowing for the exaggeration to be found in all nocturnal visitations—he had little difficulty in recognizing the two gentlemen who had been staying at the Hall. The shorter and thicker of the visitors was conspicuous by a black thumb. So black was it, indeed, that it caught the dreamer's eye to the exclusion of other objects. As he moved about the school, apparently intent on examining the rude provisions for rustic education, he would touch with his thumb as he passed the corner of a desk or a map, or even occasionally a page of the copy-book in which some youthful student was laboriously inditing one of the good old saws of which the words (after the practice has departed) are still considered good enough to employ the pens of the first and second standards. Long before the seventh standard is reached—so precocious are young people now-a-days—the well-worn maxims of our great-grandmothers are voted antiquated and absurd. Wherever the black thumb of the stranger settled for an instant, there remained after its removal a large round black mark. After a great many of these marks had been affixed—as if they were a sort of trade-mark—all about the school, the dreamer was conscious of an expectation that each succeeding impression would become fainter than its predecessor. But this did not appear to be the case. The longer of the two strangers looked on at the performance with an expression of gratified malice. Maggie's eloquent face wore a displeased look, and it was easy to guess that her protest was only not forthcoming on account of the usual difficulty experienced by actors in a dream of saying or doing what they wish to. At last, however, the short thick gentleman got ruder or bolder, and, instead of being satisfied with marking the maps or even the copy-books, made for the young school-master himself, and attempted to affix his sign-manual. The thin stranger uttered a discordant shriek of laughter. Maggie rushed forward—and the dream was over.

There was nothing particularly pleasant in the

dream itself. The shriek had no doubt been imported from a quarrel—which might even be a renewing of love—between two cats on the roof. It was therefore the more strange that the dreamer on awaking was conscious of a happiness which the best of dreams seldom leaves behind it—a feeling that something had happened which would make life for the future worth living. Those who have felt this on awaking are to be envied in that they have felt what falls but to the lot, of very few, and pitied because they will always be wishing to feel it again. But the man who feels it only once will cease for a while wondering why he was born. It was some time before he could recall the cause of a happiness which could scarcely be attributed to his dream. Then the letter and cheque of the publisher flashed into his mind, and he turned over and went to sleep again.

Doubtless, if people—even not very kind ones— knew what great things a little kindness can do for others, and how it re-acts on the recipient, and makes the most surly anxious to do a kindness to some one in his turn, they would be less sparing of what often costs them little or nothing. Almost everybody might do something towards making the world less miserable, for the reason that if you have no real kindness to offer, simulated kindness often does as well. In fact, the latter is occasionally found the more serviceable, as it is not liable to err through an excess of zeal. But the affectation of a virtue one is wanting in is always praiseworthy as setting a good example, and also as showing a desire in the pretender for better things. There are an immense number of people who, from one motive or other, are always ready to do a kindness. But then the needy are so many. I like a man who, if he has a parrot that enjoys having his head scratched, will walk yards every morning to scratch it for him, rather than that the poor bird should feel even for a day that nobody cares for him.

Of the cheque for five guineas, which he would have kept framed over his mantelpiece if he could have afforded it—perhaps no money is ever afterwards as sweet as that first cheque: the Baron's banknotes of fabulous value are nothing to it—one shilling was expended on a copy of the magazine in which his article appeared, and this was posted at once to Beddington. Nor did it—how bold the tiny success had already made him—bear the name, though it bore the address, of the Squire. Perhaps it would be incorrect to say that no one before ever built so palatial a mansion, such a castle in Spain, on such a poor foundation. But no one could ever have built on any foundation a palace he wished more to inhabit. Of one of his heroes Bulwer-Lytton says that "from the eminence of five shillings a week he looked over the promised land." Charles Collins looked up rather at an eminence whose summit was obscured by clouds. But the hill was Parnassus—or whatever may be its modern substitute—and the difficulties of scaling it had vanished.

Perhaps he would have felt less excitement if he had known that the road, for those who have the *entrée*, is macadamized, and that the Pegasuses of those who ride up a-horseback are rather remarkable for length of ears than strength of wing.

In thinking, too, that it would be impossible to work out the new mine, Mr. Collins had fallen into a mistake to which all who have hit on a new discovery or a plagiarism of an old and half-forgotten one are especially liable. They insist on throwing an enormous quantity of their precious metals—as they consider them—on the market. The market gets glutted, and the price drops. One day the people—or those of them who care at all about the matter—to use the piteous words of the late Poet-Laureate, "take it for a weed." A weed in these times is anything that is very common. It may be never so good, but once let the new flower get so cheap that "common people" can afford to wear a second-rate specimen, and its beauty will count for very little. But the young poet was sanguine—youth that is not sanguine is good for very little—therefore he saw no limit to the profitable transmuting of verse into prose. Moreover, he slyly determined that his prose should still be poetry. If songs without words are such a success, why not poetry without rhyme or metre? He was so far right that rhyme and metre without sense, if they cannot make prose are equally incapable of true poetry.

But if the effect on the "new writer" of the five guineas was great, it was as nothing to the emotions experienced by the receiver of the magazine. Maggie, who had but few acquaintances in the literary world, at first wondered who could have taken the trouble to send it. She was sufficiently a novice to be prepared to find any article charming to which her notice was directed. She soon saw the blue pencil mark on the first page of the article entitled "An old Mill." She had not read through the second page before she had arrived at the personality of the author. More than this, she was soon aware that the "new writer" loved her. How she discovered this last was a mystery, unless indeed the pages may have acted in some way as a medium. She had got to feel quite foolish before she came to the last page of the article, which was indeed rather a commonplace one. "Such a deathless flower," she thought, as she closed the book and lay back in her chair to conjure up the pretty scene before her mind's eye, "in place of that perishable one that I gave him." At the thought she blushed redder than any rose.

It came to pass at this time that almost everybody was pleased. The Squire was relieved that Maggie was not going to marry any one. Tom Lovibond was delighted to see a chance of retaining the Squire's friendship without tying himself for life to his daughter, whom he adored. Mr. Collins was happy in the double heaven of having his first article accepted, and his first love not yet "declined with thanks." Maggie felt satisfied that she would never marry any one—not she. If quite everybody could be quite happy it would be a good world. I am afraid that too many are jealous of the happiness of others—even though they do not want it themselves —for this to be possible. To prevent things from getting altogether too monotonous, about this time the relations between Mr. McCawmee Jones and Mr. Corthee got a little strained. There is hardly any one who will allow a person whom he imagines he is serving to keep kicking him, and if constantly performed in public a good deal of self-control is required in him who undergoes the operation. In fact the Poet had been a little ruder than usual— he could not have been much ruder—and had also allowed himself to administer flagellations outside the comparative privacy of the recognized swishing-room.

There has recently been a good deal of talk about a "universal language," and no doubt there is a taking sound about it. What a truly grand thing it would be if all the many-coloured nations of the earth were able to understand one another, except in the rather frequent cases where there would be nothing to understand, or only such things as had better remain uncomprehended. I am myself of opinion that the larger portion of the human race which lives by disseminating the manufactures of an advanced civilization among those who can be convinced that they require them, would be the chief gainers by the carrying out of the new scheme, and if this is so they had better set to work and invent a language—if they have not already done so—for themselves. I should like also to point out that even those who are most convinced of the advantages that a "universal language" would confer are by no means agreed as to which would be the best language for the purpose. Welshmen, Germans, Chinese, and others who have been brought up in the enjoyment of a mellifluous and easily-written mother-tongue would naturally object to making barbarous French or English the general medium of communication. Perhaps it is the fact that nobody objects to a "universal language" as long as he has not—at an age when he may have lost all taste for philological studies—to learn a new language himself. As this would mean that everybody desires that his own language—perhaps even his own dialect—should be the chosen one, it will be seen that there is at the outset a considerable divergence of opinion.

Very often, when sages and philosophers have been disputing about some question for ages, a babe or comparative suckling has hit upon a solution which they in their excitement have overlooked. This appears to have been the case with the "universal language." In reality a substitute for all this suggested philology has been in existence from the remotest ages. It has the advantage of requiring no dictionary and no grammar, and of being independent of colleges and "professors"; while it is as readily comprehended, and, I may add, communicated, by the deaf and dumb as by others. Of course, like every other good thing, it has its drawback, and there are some effeminate people in this effeminate age who persist in saying that it is lacking in delicacy and refinement. Possibly there are a few millions on whom these would be completely thrown away.

The "universal language," which will not in our day be superseded, is a strong boot, with a foot in it, and impelled by a vigorous leg. Its unsparing use gained for the great Bismarck the empire and his fame, and by it Englishmen, to whom the very meaning of philology is unknown, are to-day making colonies in every quarter of the world. In the every-day affairs of life equally with great national questions it exerts an overpowering influence, and the one drawback is that those who comprehend it best object most strongly to its employment. For this reason it is perhaps wise not to venture on the use of the "universal language," unless—as was the case with Bismarck—your boot is a very stiff one. The Poet was fond—as we all are—of speaking in a language in which he fancied himself a proficient.

The Critic, who was a bit of a philologist, under-stood the language as well as anybody, and had lately been having a good deal of metaphorical "boot." He began to enter into the feelings of Iarbas when he threatened to cease placing sacrifices on the altars he had erected to Jupiter, since little or no profit was derived from the transaction. Iarbas no doubt had a turn for satire which Jove may have relished or not, but he was at a disadvantage compared with Mr. Jones in that it was almost impossible in those days to start a new religion to spite a deity that had spurned you. There are very few who can do this now, but Mr. Jones thought he was one of the few. If he was incapable he felt that it was not for want of practice. He made up his mind one night when he had been rubbed very much the wrong way to make no more sacrifices at Mr. Corthee's altar, or even to accept his benefactions—the Poet occasionally chucked him an invitation to dinner—any more. The announcement of Mr. Collins's new book (though the manuscript had occasioned a little friction between old Mr. Wadhams and the Critic) appeared to be a favourable opportunity for the erecting of a new altar.

CHAPTER XXII.

THE KING IS DEAD.

THERE is no doubt that the unfortunate Poet's peculiarities laid him open to any enemy who had once been a friend, and had enjoyed the privileges of intimacy which make it so easy to turn an old ally into a laughing-stock. It is to be feared that modern minor poets—my hero, who is going to blossom into a minor poet so soon, is of course an exception—belong as a rule to the vast army whom no irresistible impulse from within forces to take up the pen. This fact is doubtless to be deplored, and yet very agreeable writers may have started without anything to say and ended by finding a good deal. Not to go too far, it is surely a mistake to start on your journey with your basket crammed with flowers you have bought, a little faded perhaps, at the shop, and so be unable to find room for the fresher ones you may meet with by the wayside. Of course the man who has only a basket to begin with—which may be considered equivalent to the binding of a book—may come in at evening without any flowers at all. A great deal depends on the country through which your road passes, and there are plenty of people who travel from Dan to Beersheba and find all barren—as might very possibly be the case with me ; but then I won't travel that road. Still, it seems that only an entire absence of humour could account for any one's beginning to write a book without having anything to say. As soon might we expect to find a painter starting on a sketching tour without any paints. Of the latter we might safely prophesy that he would not be hung on the line. Oddly enough, the same failure cannot confidently be predicted for the former.

It sounds absurd—as do a great many things heard for the first time—but there is no doubt that if everybody had a sense of humour there would be an end to all fun. As it is there is no great amount remaining, and a goodly portion of what is left is due to the self-importance and solemnity of a number of people—to whom we can never feel sufficiently grateful—who cannot tell when you are laughing at them. Now Mr. Jones had always found it impossible to keep from laughing—inward laughter, of course, as laughing outright would have gone near to killing the goose whose egg if not golden had yet a certain value—to see the Poet working early and late (for no one could be more industrious) at his hashes and *réchauffés* of old poets, of whose existence he fondly hoped very few people were aware. Long practice had given him the knack of metres, and his compositions were always rhythmical and pleasing. It was only on examination —and this fact had enabled Mr. Jones to "run him" so successfully—that an occasional reader discovered that there was nothing in the verses at all. To Eton men they recalled the "nonsense verses" which they had been accustomed to compose when in the Lower School. Mr. Corthee's high and mighty air had given Mr. Jones many a merry moment at times when circumstances did not greatly excite, except in the case of a Mark Tapley, to joviality. These happy moments he had enjoyed none the less that to share his sensations with another would have been to spoil trade. Joy is not always a twin, and I have never heard that misers were incapable of appreciating the stores which they yet did not allow to gladden the eyes of any other human being. It was something of a relief, too, to have done with the tiresome pretence of admiring that in which he saw nothing to admire. There are moments when even the most thorough humbug sighs—he does not often get much farther—to be genuine.

It is not my purpose to relate very exactly the way in which Mr. Jones, having once made up his mind, proceeded to let down the Poet. There are plenty of people already who are sufficiently well versed in the useful art of dropping a friend. This must occasionally be done even by the most steadfast of men. We are all liable to change, and you or your friend may change so much and so rapidly that it becomes necessary for one or other to retire from the firm. I am comforted when it is the other who first grows weary of the partnership. Mr. Jones was much too skilful to act with startling abruptness. He began by adulterating the praise (which gradually became fainter) with little doubts and innuendoes which his position of anonymous critic gave him every opportunity of inserting. It was not indeed the first time that he had been obliged to repudiate an article of his own manufacture. His procedure was perfectly comprehended of the *cognoscenti*, some of whom may even have suffered the same thing at the hands of some other performer. These latter lost no time in following the golden rule, " to do as you

R

are done by." They copied Mr. Jones's action as if
they were sheep going through a gap, till, shortly,
Mr. Corthee found himself being looked on quite
coldly. He had never had any personal popularity
to lose, having felt so secure of his position that it
had not seemed worth his while to affect friendship
with more than two or three. Perhaps for this
reason the " Immortals " found the less difficulty in
convincing themselves of his exceptional mortality.
After the first whimper or two the whole pack
opened on him speedily. A review or two, into
whose pages he was imported—like a nine-pin, or an
Aunt Sally—for the purpose of being knocked down,
and of which no one appeared to be able to guess the
authorship, put a finish to his career, and one
morning the "Poet of the ages "—as he had been so
recently termed—awoke to find himself, poetically
speaking, a dead corpse. Perhaps he was more
unfortunate than Othello, in that his "occupation"
remained. He became more laborious than ever,
and the less people cared for his work, the more
care and polish did he bestow on it. It was almost
a pathetic sight—or would have been if any
spectators had been admitted—to behold him pain-
fully putting the finishing touches, by the light of
the midnight lamp, to poems never destined to see

the light of day. But indeed his work had always smelt of the candle. Of such writers it need only be said that some candles smell better than others.

But the necessity for praising some one was innate in Mr. Jones's breast, and, having finished with his late ally, he proceeded to transfer his bland and unctuous worship to Mr. Collins's little book, which indeed appeared to merit his encomiums. The new poet—how delightful to be told by the anonymous bestower of immortality that one is "the new poet" —took the praise thankfully, and without any suspicion of the motives which had in the first place made him its recipient. He actually—the fact is worth recording—made a little money by his book. It ran rapidly through two editions—not very large ones—and was now going rather slowly through the third, when the young author was surprised to find, from an invitation to dinner which lay one morning on his breakfast table, that the Squire and his daughter were in London.

Maggie, of course, had been the first person to receive a copy of the new poet's "works," inscribed "with the author's compliments." She commenced the perusal of this second missive with feelings that surprised her, although she had discovered from the first one that she was not insensible. This time the

book was almost certainly sentient, and to read it was
to talk to the author.   To talk to him too as she had
never talked to him before, and in a way that she
would never before have dreamt that he was capable of
appreciating.   Her brief and unpromising experience
of authors—in the flesh—had not entirely destroyed
all reverence for the few who do well what she was
unable to persuade herself that she could do at all.
We should' be exceedingly thankful that a love for
the occupations and amusements of country life—not
to mention the more exciting town life—with steam-
yachts, race-horses, cricket, and a few other matters
of absorbing interest, have made it impossible for
everybody to write.   Although a poet of old was
reported to write his poems "standing on one foot,"
there are no doubt positions which militate against
the practice of writing, to say nothing of composing.
Only exceptional individuals could write anything
which should be worth reading, or even legible, during
the qualms of sea-sickness, or while engaged in the
pursuit of the fox.   Indeed the want of any regular
occupation may be looked on as one of the chief
incentives to the writing not only of poems.   No
doubt boredom has contributed more than its fair
quota to the ranks of literary aspirants, and it must
be allowed that the writings of a man who, like

Solomon, has been prodigiously bored, are not seldom found to be instructive as well as amusing.

Maggie had been in possession of the charmed book but a few days, during which time she read and re-read it to the neglect of other and perhaps healthier occupations, when she began gently—as her way was—to tease her father into going to London. Certainly it was the season, of which a part was generally spent in town; but this year it had been somehow decided that they should go elsewhere. The good Squire had no greater pleasure in life than to please his daughter, and after wondering for a while that Maggie should be so anxious to transfer herself to the smoky city which she was always so eager to leave after a few days, he consented as a matter of course. He had a little house in the neighbourhood of —— Square, which he sometimes let, but which was, fortunately for Maggie's comfort, unoccupied, and for this they started a few days after her wishes became known. No sooner had they settled down after their migration than the Squire was informed that he ought to give a dinner-party.

"A dinner-party!" he exclaimed—no suggestion of Maggie's ever moved him to anything approaching vexation. "Who on earth am I to give a dinner-party to, I should like to know? I know nobody I should care to ask, or who if asked would care to come. Certainly old Leatherhead is in town "— Leatherhead was the county member—" but it is his place, I should think, to ask me. Not that I want him to though."

"You might ask our old friends, Mr. Corthee and Mr. Jones," said Maggie shyly.

"I did not know you were so smitten with them," said the Squire, raising his eyebrows. "Even so, two people won't make a dinner-party. It would be quite enough to ask them to lunch, or, if you are so anxious to have them, to afternoon tea. Can't say I care much about them myself."

Maggie moved to the fire-place, and turning her back on her father, placed her elbows on the mantelpiece and her chin in her hands. If she had looked at herself in the mirror, which she was careful to avoid doing, she would have seen that her cheeks were turning to a bright rosy red. The Squire of course could see nothing; so that perhaps no one was aware that Maggie was blushing.

"You might ask Mr. Collins," she said, without raising her eyes. "It might be a good thing for him to meet people."

"Hum!" said the Squire. "I should be pleased, of course—a very decent young chap. I don't suppose, though, that he has a dress suit. If he has he only makes three. And how he is to get any good from meeting those others I can't imagine. More likely to get sneered at for his pains."

Perhaps it was rather disingenuous of Maggie to commence by suggesting the Poet and the Critic, both of whom she rather disliked. She had, too, a conviction—had it been supplied to her by the new book ?—that neither wished well to Mr. Collins. But can a young woman always be ingenuous ? It must be remembered that Maggie was not in the least aware of whither she was tending. Poets—she had not as yet come across many of them—were not in her estimation to be treated like ordinary beings. They were very different from village school-masters.

The Squire began to rack his brains to remember a few Daneshire people whom he could invite to the proposed feast. Having failed in this effort, a bright idea dawned upon him.

" I will go this afternoon," he said, " to the ' Immortals.' They were very civil to me last year. I dare say I can find a few men there whom I know. Now you see what you've let yourself in for. You'll have to entertain a lot of young fellows—for I can't —and I wish you well through it."

Maggie laughed, as well she might. She had not

yet had much cause to distrust her powers of entertaining " young fellows," and indeed—so modest was
she—had been more than once surprised at the ease
with which it was done. It seemed sufficient to
smile and look pleasant.

The Squire went forth on his voyage of discovery.
" Bother the little puss," he was saying to himself as
he walked up the dingy steps, and was admitted
through the narrow portal into the sacred precincts
of the " Immortals." The dilapidated hall-porter—
there was no hall—arrayed in a worn and frayed
livery of sky-blue, informed him that Mr. Jones was
within, and a youth was summoned to show the way
to the smoking-room. The place, to the Squire's
eye, looked nearer dissolution, and so perhaps to
Immortality, than on his last visit. The walls of the
narrow passage that ran from the front door to the
foot of the stairs were thickly lined with coats of
every make and material, intended no doubt to exag-
gerate and display, or in some few cases to hide the
peculiarities of their owners. All sorts of outer
coverings were there, from the many-caped and
voluminous mantle which might have served a
poetical cabman, down to the merest and lightest
apology for an overcoat. The hats too were of every
shape and fashion, from the velvet billycock of the

poet, who felt that his hat should not be as other men's, to the curly-brimmed top hat of one who had not yet received the encouragement which would justify him in cutting himself adrift from other than " Immortal " society. Hebe, in the form of a foolish scullion, was removing from the dining-room dishes and glasses, presumably with remnants of the modern substitutes—in appearance not very appetizing—for nectar and ambrosia.

High up in the attics was situated the smoking-room, and here Mr. Jones was at last run to ground. He was alone, except for a brandy-and-soda, and half asleep in an arm-chair when aroused by the entrance of the visitor. His face had been wearing a hipped and discontented expression—as of a middle-aged Tithonus—which was changed for a look of pleasure as he recognized the Squire.

"You, Mr. Ellis? of all people," he exclaimed, rising quickly and extending his plump hand. "Who would have dreamt of seeing you in town? I am truly delighted. And how is Miss Ellis ? "

A greeting evidently so genuine in its friendliness had the natural effect of making the Squire in his turn feel more friendly than he had intended. He had scarce got his cigar well alight before he had broached the subject of Maggie's dinner-party. The

Critic at once accepted the invitation with quite evident eagerness. " By George ! " he was thinking, " I should rather imagine I would go. If it hadn't been for that idiot of a Poet there is no saying what might not have happened. She was awfully nice to me. I wonder if I am quite forgotten." He was unmindful of the fact that until the Squire's unexpected appearance Maggie had been lately consigned to oblivion.

Mr. Jones set himself at once to provide the required guests, who, if respectable, he was determined should neither be too handsome nor too brilliant. He was at first a little perplexed by the Squire's disinclination to have " any more of those poets."

" But we are all poets here," Mr. Jones had said, " or very nearly so."

" Then," the Squire replied, "I must go elsewhere."

The matter was compromised later in the afternoon by the acceptance of some young men of whom the ˙Critic was able to affirm that to the best of his knowledge they had not written anything, and had certainly published nothing. They were, he explained, *in statu pupillari*—mere hewers of eulogy, and drawers of admiration. The Squire was taken with their manners, which were as yet unaffected; and Mr. Jones was satisfied in that they were neither clever nor good-looking—in fact, one of them had a decided squint. They appeared, as they doubtless felt, surprised at receiving an invitation to dinner from a stranger after a few minutes' conversation in a club smoking-room, but their awe of the Critic—as one whose services they intended one day to utilize—induced them civilly to accept.

The Squire returned home in capital spirits. He was always happy when he had done anything that he thought would please Maggie.

He was received with a kiss which, to his surprise, was no warmer than usual, when he related the success of his mission, and his daughter seemed to have forgotten all about the dinner-party, as to which she could not be induced to say a word. The Squire stared and wondered, but had all his life been too unobservant of such matters to be able to explain her sudden coolness. He went to bed feeling, as he put it, that he had made an old fool of himself.

" Bother the little puss !" he muttered to himself as he went up-stairs. "I can't make head or tail of her."

In course of post a rather cool note of acceptance arrived from his *quondam* school-master. The Squire had expected something more grateful and gushing, but he held his peace as Maggie seemed perfectly satisfied. Mr. Corthee politely declined. He would have liked much to meet his cousin again, but had no wish to do so in the company of Mr. Jones, whom he had got to hate with a vehemence which would have been useful to his art, which had for the most part to get on without any such impulse. Maggie's " image," however, had never ceased to be present with him. But for the ridiculous scene in the garden, when the striped knicker-bockers of his then friend and critic had appeared at the opposite door, there was no saying how far his " passion " might have carried him. He had since seen, of course, that such a sudden declaration would have been absurd, and must have resulted in a refusal. He had intended to pay another visit to Daneshire, on the " kill or cure " principle, but had never yet found the necessary courage. A second sight of the one who at first sight took one captive, frequently, no doubt, acts as a release. You are in a different humour, or, more probably, she is; or that legacy from your, or her, aunt was not forth-coming; or her eyes are not quite so bright as you fancied them, or—well, you see the folly of it. It is odd that it is never the impossibility of these things that one sees. It was exceedingly doubtful, however, whether, in the exceptional case of Maggie, a second visit would not have the effect of causing the captive to fall into still more hopeless captivity. This probability was not overlooked by the Poet, who at the present crisis in his fortunes was anxious to avail himself of any promising material for his mill. He had done his best to make the first occasion of their meeting useful in his profession, and had indeed worked up the description of his imaginary torments in language which even Dante would have found it difficult to improve on. He was faintly aware that he had made a mistake in leaving out Maggie. He would see what he could do with her when he met her again. In the meantime he cursed his cowardice in leaving her to "that fellow Jones."

CHAPTER XXIII.

THE CRITIC IS MAGNANIMOUS.

THE day of the Squire's dinner-party duly arrived, and the ex-school-master was the first of the guests to put in an appearance. Though he had answered the Squire's note so coolly, he had been ever since its receipt in a state of feverish joy and anticipation quite becoming to a poet. Absence had certainly not had on him the healing effect with which it is so often credited—but it is the women perhaps to whom it ministers. Besides his anticipated meeting with Maggie he had another reason for happiness which would have caused his not very hopeful landlady, had she been aware of it, to discard him for ever. In the *Standard* of that morning had appeared a long and appreciative review of his book, to the new poet's intense surprise. So lavish, indeed, was the praise, that Mr. Collins, who for a poet had yet quite a fair amount of modesty, felt shocked. Who was he to be placed on a pedestal high above all others? He was unaware, in his innocence, that these promotions are often made from motives which have very little to do with either rhyme or reason, and that the promoted one is not infrequently deposed even more suddenly than he was exalted. It must be his merit, he thought, which had made him, as he considered it, famous. Doubtless there were worthy men on the look-out for genius—he blushed at the word—and all that was said of the jealous and unkind ways of critics must be untrue.

He had just time to exchange greetings with Maggie and her father when Mr. Jones was ushered in. He looked so different from the Mr. Jones of the red knickerbockers that Mr. Collins did not recognize him in the least; nor on his side had the Critic the slightest recollection of the young man whom he had met for a few minutes in the village school. On the Squire's introducing them, Mr. Jones of course became aware that he was in the presence of his most recent creation. He looked on the young man with some pride, and as a tailor may survey the client whom he considers he has made —as no doubt very often happens—by his skill. He at once took on the genial, fatherly manner which he reserved for his new clients. Most of these, while they resented the patronizing air, were aware of the service which had evoked it. In fact Mr. Jones was not accustomed to hide his light under a bushel. It was never very long before the astonished deity was informed of the personality of the head-worshipper—the author, so to speak, of the new religion. Mr. Collins, however, was puzzled at Mr. Jones's air of proprietorship. "He means well, no doubt," he was thinking; "but what a bore the fellow is." The Critic was beaming on him like the good uncle in a play. He had intended by his review merely to give the finishing blow to Mr. Corthee, but he would not refuse the credit of having performed a kind action at the same time. So this was the young school-master he had met at Beddington. A slight feeling of uneasiness came over him as he recalled the look the school-master had given him as he entered the school. He had afterwards thought it absurd to put this down to jealousy, but here was the young man again, and it was impossible to say how often Maggie and he might not have met lately. He talked for a few minutes to his latest creation. "You will do now," were his words as he moved away.

He was strengthened in his idea that Maggie and

young Collins must have met frequently by the assurance with which the latter came forward on the announcement of dinner with the offer of his arm. Here was a change indeed! Charles Collins was not in the least conscious of any presumption, of which he was one of the last to be willingly guilty. But he simply could not keep away. Mr. Jones could not perceive any reluctance in Maggie to her escort, and it would have been hard to see what she certainly was very far from feeling. Mr. Jones contented himself, since he could get no better, with taking the seat on her other hand. No sooner had dinner commenced than Maggie and her other neighbour began to converse. Mr. Jones listened with all his ears, and was rewarded by the discovery that the conversation was very commonplace indeed. Unfortunately he had not the clue which might have enabled him to read between the lines. When Maggie asked in a low voice, "How do you like London?" she meant—though she knew it not—"Have you forgotten Beddington? What a time it seems since you left it!" When he replied that he liked London—how he hated it a week ago!—he meant, "I love it now that I am sitting beside you." To the young man's poetic sense the contact, the touch of the gauzy white dress was simply enthralling.

Mr. Jones was quite as near on the other side—
even closer, as he bulged more over his chair—but
he felt nothing, and may possibly have been surprised and vexed at the discovery. As he found,
from the few words that reached him, that they had
not met since the young school-master left Beddington, he was puzzled to account for the evident
understanding between them. They were for the
most part silent. So also was Mr. Jones, but his
time was well occupied in discussing the excellent
dinner. Maggie and Mr. Collins, though they were
so silent, did not apparently require earthly food.
Mr. Jones began to think the dinner a bore, for indeed
to a man of his sort no silence can ever be very
golden. Even to other people it must be the silence
of the girl you love and who is sitting near you.
Of course there are people, not very old ones either,
who prefer their dinner—when it is a good one—to
all else. When at last Maggie repented of what she
considered her rudeness, and turned guiltily to talk
to the Critic, the latter chose to feel annoyed by and
ignore her conversation.

"I might have saved my labour," he was thinking.
"Confound the fellow, I have given him a leg up and
no mistake." But his disgust was not of long con-
tinuance. Maggie persisted in her efforts to soothe

him—she was not without an inkling of the state of affairs—and a good dinner, combined with a certain amount of deference paid one by a charming girl, will work wonders. By degrees he began to smile to himself. When Maggie left the room he had never seemed in a more genial mood. "I'll be good-natured and help him," he was saying to himself. He turned the conversation to the new book, and so praised it to the skies that the Squire began to think his ex-school-master the greatest genius under heaven. The young man listened in a state of confused wonder. Could this be so? Was it all true, and true of him? If any doubts of the Critic's sincerity troubled him, they were put aside as we put aside all opinions—especially our own—with which it is convenient to disagree. As the young literary-men-to-be who were present chimed in with wishes for success that they felt sure were deserved, he longed to make the round of the table and shake hands with his new and fervent admirers.

Mr. Jones took leave rather early, and walked home alone, not feeling particularly jovial, but having accepted the inevitable. "That ass the Poet" would be out of it too. He decided he did not really want a wife. What should he do with a wife? Maggie would object to appearing in the photographers' windows. How could he give up his club? It would be a burning shame to leave Maggie alone, and go off to a club. Sour grapes; no doubt, but the fox really thought them sour. Maggie's manner too was a little provincial. She would want him to hunt; no more of that, thank you. He wondered how young Collins would like it. Altogether there were sufficient reasons for generosity. As he took out his latch-key he was able to contemplate the possibility of uttering, at no very distant date, the time-honoured formula, "Bless you, my children."

261

CHAPTER XXIV.

LONG LIVE THE KING.

No Radical wire-puller could have worked harder
to secure the election to Parliament of an incapable
windbag than did Mr. Jones to obtain recognition
for the newest and only poet. In doing so he was
—as is generally found to be the case—actuated by
mixed motives. Of these, as the best are seldom
without alloy, the worst are seldom altogether mean.
No doubt the chief motive—without which indeed
the others might not have come into operation—was
to spite Mr. Corthee. He was also anxious to prove
—if only to himself—that he was unhurt by Maggie's
evident preference for the new lion. But besides
these he was moved by a really genuine wish to be
of service to a lover, even if not yet accepted, of
whose position he almost persuaded himself he was
not envious. The frequency with which the prac-
tised critic had elevated to the front rank unfortunate

poets (whom he had shortly discovered reasons for deposing) made the operation easier to him than would have been the shelling of the proverbial peas. The enormous number of reviews and notices that appeared almost simultaneously was as remarkable as the similarity of the terms in which they were indited. Indeed any voracious reader who should have been so fortunate as to make acquaintance with them all would have been of opinion that if there was—as appeared to be the case—but one poetical creed, so also was there but one prophet of the new religion. Notices of "the new poet" for that season took the place of gigantic gooseberries, and of toads—whose rocky places of sepulture penny-a-liners seemed to have lost the knack of discovering. In fact a good many people got bored. Not however before they had been worried into buying the new book, which soon became the fashion. Perhaps to be over-praised is as demoralizing as to be undervalued. There is the sure and inevitable reaction when the very people who were loudest in singing your praises are the first to proclaim that they have been imposed on. So they have been perhaps—and by themselves.

It may be doubted whether Mr. Collins was sufficiently worldly-wise to see the advisability of taking

pigs to market before they fell in value, but the
reaction would not be yet, and in the meantime he
rode gaily on the top of the wave. He saw a good
deal of Maggie in these days. Whether the Squire
had an idea that poets differed from common people,
in that they were incapable of feeling the passion of
which they chiefly discoursed, is uncertain. He was
wrong if he supposed that his old *protégé* had any
insuperable objection to being further introduced to
feelings of which his writings proved him to be not
without some knowledge. But the lovers did. not
approach one another as rapidly as might have been
expected from the strength of the first attraction.
There are positions—or larks seem to think so—in
which it is pleasing to hover motionless with ex-
tended wings. It is doubtful whether any rapture
to be experienced afterwards will surpass or equal
the first timid, bashful admittance of the new joy.
At first, and while one at least may be in ignorance
of the full meaning of the new sensations, there is
an approach towards heaven which mortals not often
rise to. Hover on poised wings while ye may, ye
lovers ; the nest to which you will descend is on the
ground.

But the time came when the Squire got tired to
death of London, and when even the reflected glory

of having a poet about the house, who had once been his village school-master, did not compensate for the loss of country air. He began to feel that he would gladly give up all these delights to be leaning once more over the door of the pig-sty at the Home Farm, scratching with his stick the backs of those lovely little Berkshires, who would by this time have grown out of all knowledge. Even if he was not to be allowed to go home, it was absolutely necessary, he felt, that he should go to some place a little more like the country than was London in the season.

Possibly Maggie was answerable for the choice— instead of a return to Beddington—of a watering-place not so remote from the great city but that it would be easy for a friend, should he wish to do so, to run down on Saturday and stay till Monday. The Squire made no objection, though had the matter been left to him, he might have wished to go further afield. I have my doubts whether he was quite as innocent as he appeared to be of the point to which affairs were tending. At this time I imagine that he was a little dazzled with all the honour and glory that the reviews were piling upon his young friend. He knew little of literary society, or of the causes—frequently quite independent of literary merit or the reverse—which elevate to or depose from the pinnacles of Fame. He must surely have seen something, though it is the custom of the British father to shut his eyes to these things. It mattered little, for if he thought about the matter at all, it was probably to decide not to think about it—at present.

He was not one of those who like thinking, or who —except in very exceptional cases—see any good at all in the habit. Thinking about an evil—yet he would not call it an evil—which you cannot possibly prevent is the most foolish thinking of any. ' He only knew that he had never refused Maggie anything, and that he was not going to begin now. What he should do at Gaybeach, where there were no amusements at all, he could not imagine. Perhaps when they arrived there he would have to think. He preferred to take things as they came. The selection by an immortal of a consort from among the daughters of men was no doubt of old considered as flattering as it generally proved dangerous to the object. If his daughter intended offering herself a willing sacrifice there would be little chance that any attempt of his would dissuade her, and the less that the attempt would never be made. He would make up his mind—as those dreadful old stoics used

to accept these little matters—to the deprivation.
Yet it was hard—it would be hard—to lose his pet.
Perhaps he may be pardoned—he was getting into
years—for thinking that in the end it would be
harder for the pet. Yet Maggie after all might elect
to stay with him. Even so there are pets—pet
lambs, for example—which are taken away against
their wills. He began to wonder that he had never
thought of this before. He was not a man—he
supposed—to be affected by sufferings which did
not touch him or his. We are indeed accustomed
to take with equanimity—if not altogether without
interest—the tragedies that effect the lives of others.
So it happened that, on their way to Gaybeach, the
Squire and his daughter found themselves at Vic-
toria Station with—owing to having missed a train,
which also was owing to Maggie's dilatoriness over
her packing—two hours to spare.

Though waiting at the crowded station was tedious
work, the Squire could not help thinking that it was
probably far livelier than any adventures he would
encounter at the seaside. But what on earth was
to be done? Maggie and he had partaken of a
hurried lunch before leaving, but rather than stand
about doing nothing for two hours, he would lunch
again. When he suggested their doing so, Maggie

at first rebelled, but taking pity afterwards on her father she went with him into the empty dining-room, having first vowed that she would not be tempted to eat anything. And indeed the temptations, to one who was not in the least hungry, were not very overpowering. The meats, sodden with perpetual stewings, were more provocative of dyspepsia than appetite, and even the Squire's knife and fork were soon idle. Just as he was in the act of laying them down, Maggie and he were aware of some animal that ran hastily across the room and took, as it were, refuge under the table at which they were seated. There was a pattering as of little hoofs on the uncarpeted floor. The Squire stooped to look under the table; as he did so the waiter rushed up with his napkin under his arm, and the carver threw down his knife and fork, and came hurriedly from behind his bar. They were joined by the cook, who rushed, in a breathless state of excitement, from the inner regions, and the three together stooped down in the corner of the room adjoining the Squire's table. After a rather prolonged scuffle, during which sounds were heard as of a child in distress, the three retired triumphantly, bearing aloft in procession the prettiest little white pig, with just one little brown spot over one of his little pink eyes. He looked as clean as a new pin. It was a strange pet, thought the Squire, yet doubtless he could be trained into a very learned and intelligent one. Just as the pet was disappearing with his bearers through the open door, from whence he had scampered forth so hopefully, to the Squire's surprise the little pig uplift his voice and wept. Was it imagination, or did the little pink eye glance in Maggie's direction in mute and, alas! ineffectual appeal? "Is this to happen," the look seemed to ask, "in a Christian country?"

The Squire would have thought no more of the occurrence had not the necessity of killing time brought him once more into the dining-room about an hour afterwards. While he stood by the door looking up at the clock, which admonished him that his train would soon be leaving, the cook brought in a new dish—two or three diners had just made their appearance—and the carver came forward, flourishing his knife, and removed the cover. The Squire glanced, with the critical eye of one who had dined already, to see what fare had been provided for the new-comers. Seated on the dish, in a posture of repose, smoking hot, with a lemon in his mouth, and surrounded by a sea of gravy, was the little white pig with one brown spot over his left eye. He looked round, but Maggie was not in sight. "Iphigenia," he muttered, " was nothing to this." It was strange how he was affected by the incident. At least he determined that he would not act the part of the cruel waiter, or the still more cruel carver. As long as Maggie chose to stay with him she should not be sacrificed to anybody.

CHAPTER XXV.

MAGGIE IS WITNESS TO A LOVE SCENE.

WHEN the Squire and his daughter arrived at
Gaybeach, the former found the place even duller
than he had anticipated, but he had made up his
mind not to grumble. He attached himself to
Maggie more like an elderly lover than a mere
father, and it was impossible that she could avoid
being touched by a show of affection of which she
may have comprehended the motive. " If you are
going to leave me," it meant, "it shall not be because
you do not know how much I wish you to stay."
The energy that he manifested in the pursuit of
amusement had the effect of very quickly bringing
them to the end of all possible excursions on the
land-side. Even his desire to please Maggie could
not overcome his hatred of the sea.

One Saturday afternoon he hired a dog-cart and
drove Maggie over to Bishom, an amphibious village

on a creek a few miles off, which he had been told was worth seeing. In front of the old inn where they put up was a common with the usual geese. On the edge of the common a schooner was being built, the process being partly carried on beneath the spreading boughs of an enormous oak. A number of farm-labourers were, very deliberately—as their nature is—unloading coal from a smack. In front of the inn ran a clear stream bordered with water-cresses. The stream turned a water-mill before joining the brackish waters of the creek. No doubt this would be one of the last mills to cling to the use of the generally superseded mill-stones. In a few years parsons will have to forego the well-worn texts in which mention of these occur, and to discard some ancient sermons when they come to the top of the "tub," but what moral prophets and others will be able to draw from American imported steel-rollers is hard to say. To the right of the water-mill was a farm-yard with the usual buildings, through the gaps in which appeared glimpses of water instead of green fields. The eye everywhere came on something unexpected. In the misty distance could be seen the low land which bordered the creek, and the little trees which looked like men walking at the edge of the water. Behind the old inn was an older church among tall elms. It had a quaint brick porch, which will doubtless be "restored" one day. Inside—though the Squire was unaware of the fact —was buried a daughter of Canute, whose figure, as represented on her tombstone, was of somewhat remarkable shape, and of no very striking beauty. Possibly it was by the shore of this creek that Canute rebuked the legendary flatteries of his courtiers. So slowly did the tide come in that the courtiers—to say nothing of the royal moralist— must have had occasion for the exercise of considerable patience.

As the Squire and his daughter were standing with their backs to the creek, looking across the common at the church and the tall elms which might have been a hundred miles inland, a man came out of the farm-yard with a yoke on his shoulders, which supported on each side a full pail of milk. The farm-labourer was dressed like a sailor, in high sea-boots and blue jersey. With his blue eyes and red beard he might have been—perhaps was—a descendant of Canute. After the fashion of sailors on shore he seemed to think that land business could not be done in too leisurely a manner. He sat down, without unhooking his pails or taking the yoke from his shoulders, on a big log of timber which appeared to have been diverted from its original shipbuilding purpose in order that it might make a rustic seat for the neighbourhood, and looked dreamily across the creek. It seemed almost as if he was waiting for the cream to rise, but there was perhaps more method in his laziness than is generally the case. He had not been seated for more than ten minutes or so with his large red hands still clasping the handles of the pails which stood one on each side of his knees, when the door of one of the cottages on the other side of the brook opened slowly, and a young woman with a tin can in her hand came out. She sauntered slowly towards the log of timber— all the while as if she was in reality going some other way—and seating herself at the end opposite to that which was occupied by the amphibious-looking milkman, began to twist her can about in the sun. She too looked straight across the creek, but it is doubtful whether she saw anything. Her companion—about five yards off—stole one look at her (of which she was perfectly cognizant) and then resumed contemplation—perhaps not very genuine— of his enforced substitute for the ocean. The Squire looked at Maggie with a smile on his lips. Maggie was wistfully regarding the couple on the log. It was as if they had chosen their places with a view

T

to "see-saw," and were waiting for some one to come and balance the log. Maggie was thinking that if this was "courting," it was carried on in a way which erred on the side of quietness. It is hard to look on at a game badly played, and at which we consider we should be capable of shining, without feeling a wish to enter the arena and improve on the perform-ance. If Maggie, the Squire was thinking, was only wooed in this calm fashion, there would be no great harm done. He had no fear that Maggie would be won without the importation of a little more energy. And yet, truth to say, the red-bearded man's pro-cedure bore no slight resemblance to the way in which he had done his own wooing. After a minute or two, during which the possible descendant of Canute made no more advance than the log on which he was sitting, the young woman suddenly moved a little nearer and held out her can. Probably it was in this way that the little game was always played. In fact the spectators had an impression as of previous rehearsals. The milkman of course put out his left hand to take the can, and this movement apparently imposed on the young woman the neces-sity of coming a little nearer. Then—and the per-fecting of this manœuvre must have taken consider-able practice—his right arm stole round her waist, he drew her nearer still, stooped over and kissed her, while with his left hand he dipped the little can into the pail that stood on his far side. The little idyll was getting vastly more interesting. Maggie blushed—I wonder why—as the young woman took back her full can without any perceptible attempt at wriggling her waist out of the clasp of the young milkman's arm, and set it down on the other side of her. For a few minutes they sat perfectly still, and then the red moustache and beard came down upon the young woman's face again. When they were at last taken off she moved a little away, gave her head a toss and a shake, settled her hair, put aside the young man's arm—which else might have grown there—rose slowly, took up her can, and went home across the brook. When she had been gone two or three minutes the sailor wiped his mouth with the back of his hand, rose with his pails—he had never parted from the latter; a warning perhaps of what the young woman (who had parted so readily with her can) might one day expect—and went his way.

On their return to Gaybeach it seemed natural that the Squire and Maggie should see Mr. Collins standing at the door of their house, and looking anxiously down the street. Probably from having had his wits sharpened and his memory awakened

by the little scene at the creek, the Squire watched
the young man closely as he came forward to greet
them.   He came to the conclusion that there was
nothing especially noticeable, but this comforted
him but slightly, since to the young woman at the
creek the greeting would probably have appeared
unduly obstreperous.   He blamed himself, too late,
for having been so weak as to give what he remembered was quite a cordial invitation.   But, indeed,
the men who are most in the habit of giving cordial
invitations—in order temporarily to get rid of you—
are the very people who most sincerely repent of
their weakness when the time arrives for meeting
the promissory note.   Unless the visitor had formed
the plan for his own happiness with which he was
credited by the Squire, would he have made his
appearance so soon ?   Maggie was almost certainly
the attraction.   "Unless," thought Mr. Ellis, "he
has come down to see me;" but after a look at his
daughter he decided that even the young men of the
present generation were not quite so silly as that.
He had never given Mr. Collins credit for being
sillier than the majority.   It was seldom that
he gave a thought to Maggie's looks—praise of a
daughter's beauty is almost of the kind which is said
to be no recommendation—but it was impossible to

avoid seeing that she was charming, and, except for the present crisis, he had no desire she should be otherwise. For· this once she might surely have been content to appear a little less lovely. Charlie, too—no doubt it would soon be "Charlie"—something had improved him. He had always been handsome, but now—well, there was a good deal in his looks that most girls would admire, and if his looks had been less in his favour there was the fellow's mind—confound his mind! Maggie was not, of course, like "most girls." Even as the Squire tried to lay this flattering unction to his soul, he was aware of a suspicion that there was one point in which the most superior of young women differed not greatly from her inferiors.

CHAPTER XXVI.

A SEASIDE WALK.

THE next day was Sunday, and after putting in an exemplary appearance at the little church, crammed unpleasantly with residents and visitors, there was the afternoon to be got through. To people who have the fine old English objection to amusing themselves on Sundays this time is perhaps—with the exception occasionally of the evening—the dullest portion of the week. The Squire, after his unaccustomed early dinner, would have liked to go to sleep. He went as near it as he dared when he declined the walk which was the only obvious alternative. It is not too much to say that Maggie really wished for his company. To be alone with Mr. Collins was rather more than she felt prepared for. She had arrived at feeling very happy in his society, but preferred as yet that the pleasure should be shared by a third party. Three was better, or safer company, she felt, than two. She blushed when the young man asked her shyly if she would walk with him. He was careful—or thought he was—not to alarm her with any preknowledge of what he had made up his mind should occur before their return. But a hint or two could not but peep out from the blue eyes that were sparkling with no anticipation of defeat. In fact he would have been more than mortal if the praises with which he had recently been exalted had not had the effect of removing any feeling of humility with which he might once have been troubled. He felt tolerably secure of his own future, and the offer to share it with another savoured in his opinion more of generosity than presumption.

There are occasions when the blessedness of giving is not greater than that of receiving, because they are one and the same. A short time ago a country squire had seemed to him a great personage, and his daughter unapproachable by one who had been a village school-master. Squires, and their daughters, might still be the same, but he had changed. Rather his merits had been discovered—which was the same thing. Recognition raises a man more than a legacy or a baronetcy—greatly more than a knighthood. Squires are of the earth earthy.

Some sorts of fame were earthy enough too, no doubt, but the sort to which he aspired, and to which his way seemed cleared, was as much above worldly riches or position as heaven is above the earth. It would also he hoped bring, if not riches, a modest competence with it. This, he felt, would be delightful. To have the satisfaction of soaring in spirit high above money-grubbers, and yet to obtain the goal of their grimy and uninteresting toil, would be indeed to make the best—as some bishops are said to do—of both worlds. But he was thinking little about money. To do him justice he would have taken Maggie without a penny, and—so foolish was he—without having himself the prospect of earning one. And let people say what they like about prudence and all that, he is a poor lover—I grant him a very common one—who can be deterred from daring anything by a vision of patched clothes or hashed mutton—the latter a dish that well-cooked is far from despicable—or who does not remember that, should the worst come to the worst, there are palatial mansions (pending the establishment of compulsory old-age pensions) in which poor lovers whom age has overtaken will have ample time for meditating over, if not for repenting of, their folly.

As the two started for their walk the Squire

watched them from the doorstep with a wistful
look on his face such as we have seen on that of the
faithful dog whose owner had just ordered him,
rather roughly, to "go home." We are unable to
tell the exact depth of even an educated dog's
feelings, but there is no doubt that some of them
feel any slight very acutely. The Squire had the
additional pain of knowing that he had himself to
thank for the desertion which he was deploring. Or
was it a pleasure to know that he was paining himself for Maggie's sake ? Certain it is that he was
in some way comforted, for, though he turned back
to the house with a sigh, it was not a very deep
one, and as he settled down to the perusal of *The
Field*, there were no signs on his face of the anguish
which should be the portion of loving parents who
sacrifice their daughters. After a while he strolled
out into the village—for it was nothing more.
Passing one of the little houses which had been
vacated by its owner for " the season," he caught a
glimpse through the hedge of a little party—presumably not of ultra-sabbatarian views—which did
not appear to be troubled with *ennui*. On a bench
placed in the shade of a trellised cottage were comfortably seated a youthful couple, the parents, no
doubt, of the three children who were disporting

themselves on the lawn. The not very careworn progenitors were regarding, not entirely without interest, the gambols of their offspring. But the figure on which the Squire's eyes rested longest was that of a tall, very thin, and extremely melancholy-looking old gentleman—almost certainly the grand-father or great-grandfather—who was throwing himself into what seemed dangerous contortions for the children's amusement. The feat which they most loudly applauded, and the repetition of which they demanded over and over again, was the taking of three, or even four tennis-balls in his gaunt hand, and jerking them together into the air from behind his back, whence they fell in unexpected places and frequently on the delighted children's heads. As the Squire gazed at the venerable and ghostly juggler, whom he expected every moment to see fall to pieces, he wondered if a time would come when Maggie and "Charlie" would sit calmly in the shade of the house—*his* house—while he went through a performance as amusing—and dangerous—as that of which he was now a spectator. Well, even if it was to be so, so long as it gave Maggie pleasure what would his old joints matter? No doubt he would have to do something of the sort while Mr. Collins wrote his poetry. Poets, he thought sarcastically, can only juggle with words. He felt pleased that at all events his prospective son-in-law's forte was not comic verse, and that therefore he would not be likely to be "taken off," as the very laughable father-in-law, in the act of going through his performance.

He tore himself away from the suggestive tableau and passed on into the country. He walked farther than he had intended, and as he re-passed the cottage the shades of evening were falling. He looked once more through the hedge. The youthful couple had retired indoors, having probably found it chilly outside; but the ardour of the children had by no means abated, and the veteran was still unhurt, and, rather wearily as it seemed, was performing his celebrated "four-ball-trick" for perhaps the thousandth time. The Squire's features as he passed on—this time without stopping—wore a sardonic smile. He was not a humorous man, but we should be thankful that some of us are so happily constituted as to be able to appreciate the comedies in which we are, or are likely to be, the chief actors, and so may be considered fairly secure of a never-ending source of enjoyment.

Maggie and her companion started off—the former stopping once or twice to wave farewell to her father,

who was still visible on the doorstep—along the top
of the low chalk cliff, hardly worthy of the name,
which bounded the bay. They conversed in mono-
syllables, and their jejune remarks did not stray
beyond the weather, or at all events the view, in
which there was nothing in the least remarkable.
The calm expanse of ocean without a sail on its
flat bosom was not inspiriting, while on the other
side the short barley which bordered the path was
prematurely whitened by the east wind. Mr. Collins
would have been glad to enliven matters, but no
subject occurred to him save the one for the introduction of which he was rather, to his surprise,
unprepared. When the ocean and the barley-field
had been briefly discussed, a solemn silence reigned,
broken only by the occasional cry, it might almost
have been the laughter, of a gull. Not a soul was
in sight. It was as if heaven and earth had
combined—*conscius æther connubiis*—to afford the
opportunity which one at least of the two desired.
But it appeared to both that the chance would
lapse for the want of a few words. Even the greatest
derider of the long speeches in which lovers—
in fiction—indulge when " popping the question,"
must admit that something, however brief, in the
way of speech—or, in the case of deaf mutes, the

deaf-and-dumb alphabet—must be called in before
an understanding can be arrived at. Mr. Collins
was by no means the first poet whose words, except
on paper, declined to "flow apace." Though not
given to objurgation he was mildly cursing his folly
in not having prepared and committed to memory
a little speech—it need not have been in verse. His
present need would have been admirably served by
the turning of verse into prose—for the occasion.
He felt that if he could seat himself for a few
minutes at his desk, he would rise with a really
first-class and irresistible declaration. He was not
one of those who expect that all good things will be
given him, but he would have liked a little eloquence for once. Every day we see good writers
talking very poor stuff, and *vice versâ;* yet the experience profits nothing. People go on, and will go
on for ever, making absurd efforts to shine in spheres
for which they are unfitted, long after every one
else has admitted their incapacity. Yet perhaps
examples of writers who could not find a word in
the position in which Mr. Collins now found himself
are rare. It would be well for young women to
remember that fluency on these occasions is no
guarantee of sincerity. He would force himself to
speak. Once he actually began to articulate some-

thing, but at the sound of his own voice he paused abruptly. Maggie, who had a shrewd idea of his difficulty, and thought he had overcome it, stood still. She blushed; an expectant blush—how could she help it? Then her eyes laughed—how could they help that either? Soon her lips joined in. The smile, which was almost an answer to the speech which was almost uttered, did not unloose the fountain of Mr. Collins' eloquence, because there was no such stream, but it did more, it rendered it superfluous. His eyes caught the look in hers. In a moment they were both laughing—almost.

"What a moment to laugh!" some scandalized reader says, but I am of opinion that a correct version of the proposals of even quite superior people would prove vastly amusing—more especially if it were possible to compare what they had intended to say with the reality. What Mr. Collins really said was "Maggie," but he said it in a tone which she thought left little to be desired. Then he naturally put out his hand to take hers, which was of course a little coy. Then he, very boldly—but there is a time for boldness in these affairs—drew her to him, and then he very properly kissed her. After that he may have thought that a little more eloquence would be an improvement,

and this time he said, "Oh, Maggie." The "Oh !"
meant a good deal; amongst other things, that Mr.
Collins was congratulating himself on having made
a grand discovery, which he no doubt considered put
that of Columbus into the shade. Even the eloquent
silence "on a peak of Darien" was nothing to it.
He had lit on an unexpected revelation of boundless
happiness, to which the Pacific was a narrow and
shallow pool. Moreover, the new bliss was capable,
he foresaw, of being discovered again and again.
There are not many things which, without being
discoveries at all, arouse in our breasts the conviction
that we are among the world's greatest explorers.
As long as the humblest mariner can hoist his flag
on a summit which perhaps has never been sighted
from the steam-yacht of the millionaire, I don't think
he has very much to grumble at. Then, too, the
"Oh !"—if he had only known it—was a decided step
on the road towards becoming a poet. Whether Mr.
Collins is to be a true poet or not—and we shall soon
know all about this—he could certainly never become
one without having uttered that exclamation or its
equivalent. No one can overlook the new country
without being for the moment, or the hour, or the
day, or even perhaps for the month, more or less akin
to a poet. Those who have never sighted it, and yet

pretend to be poets, are miserable humbugs. Let us hope that these exceptions to the rule of " Poets all " are not very many.

Little was said during the walk home with the exception of a few more " Oh's " and a " dearest " or two. On their arrival they found that the Squire had returned from his inspection of the veteran gymnast, and the two lovers walked hand-in-hand into the room in which he had resumed his study of *The Field*. They stood in front of him looking rather sheepish. He lifted his eyes from his paper, and a very brief glance was sufficient to tell him what had occurred.

" H'm," said the Squire, to whom an old age spent in juggling with tennis-balls did not offer insuperable attractions.

CHAPTER XXVII.

A LAUREATE SPOILED.

THERE is an old-fashioned idea that a story should end with the acceptance of the hero by the heroine, and with the addition of the briefest possible account of those less important characters concerning whose future the reader may be supposed to feel a little, perhaps a very little, curiosity. The rule is surely a good one since the voyage is safely ended, and the adventures of the trimmest clipper, once she has arrived in harbour, are not wont to be very entertaining. It is true that ships after a time start on another voyage, but each of these causes the once trim clipper to get slower and shabbier. When she is sooner or later condemned to ply as a collier, in which predicament a ship in which Captain Cook once voyaged was, not many years ago, discovered, she may have many days of usefulness before her, but the romance and, alas! the beauty

U

is gone for ever. Young women differ from ships in that when they have once arrived in harbour after a prosperous voyage they—for the most part— rest contented with the experience. Even in the cases where the hero and heroine after arriving in port have to pass through dangers and troubles together, they will find, if they are true to the vows they plighted, that, shared with one we love, dangers and troubles—which none can certainly hope to evade—are diminished by one half, and sometimes— from the sheer pride of encountering them together —actually change into joys. Besides, true lovers— like other people—have but one chance. They take it, and must make the best of it. Peevish complaints to Fortune for the results of a gift for which we once prayed her—oh! so fervently—are unmanly, and worse still, uninteresting. Now that Maggie and her lover are engaged I have too much confidence in them to suppose they will ever be other than thankful, and the Squire may be trusted in time to feel a little gratitude too.

It is of the less consequence that the new poet, though he obtained the chief desire of his heart, did not succeed in all his hopes. To do so would, even in these prosaic days, be to present a target to the arrows of outrageous Fortune, which she would be unable to resist shooting at, and which from its size would be as hard to miss as a barn door. It is better to cast away some aspiration you value, hoping that it will not be washed up at your feet again. To succeed in one hope, and that the most fondly cherished, should be enough for a man who is not very greedy in this most crowded and disappointing of worlds. Besides, a lover of his art—or what he considers such—is not like other lovers, inasmuch as possession (in the shape of Fame) is not absolutely necessary to its enjoyment. You may be a painter, and yet not desire, still less obtain, the magic letters R.A., and most truly a poet and yet never have published a line. You may have written poems, and half-ashamed hidden them in your desk, or they may be hidden unpenned within your breast. The mere fact of printing them—the mere luck of finding a publisher—does not make you any more a poet. Even if they are printed and unsuccessful, or only successful for a day, the fact does not prove you incapable. He who does not keep himself, or whom others do not keep in the front, is, in these days, soon forgotten. There are so many whose interest it is to forget and be remembered. A true poet is retiring by nature, and averse to the clamorous praises even of his admirers. If he assists—cork-

screw-like—in the extraction of these, or is desirous
of any but spontaneous honours, he must lose something of his high estate. To be a poet, even if
unrecognized, is surely enough—if the minor or
minimus poet only knew it. Only a true poet can
have the " Poet's portion," which makes him independent of critics and publishers.

There are a great many brooks and very few rivers,
and some of the brooks may think they are hardly
treated. They started from as full sources, hurried
as eagerly down just the same sort of clefts into
valleys large enough to support a river ; and there
they are only poor little brooks. Who can say what
made the difference in their fortunes ? A ledge of
rock, perhaps only a stone or two, or the want of
help from another rivulet at a critical time ? What
does it matter ? It should be a consolation that if
all the brooks were rivers there would be no room for
dry land. Luckily there are brooks which think—
we will suppose for a moment that brooks think—
that their lives are the best. Dancing down from
stone to stone under the hazel-boughs, sparkling and
laughing while the big gloomy river sweeps moodily
on through the dirty towns to the sea.

It is no slight thing to be true, sincere, charitable,
to think no evil, to see something good and beautiful

where others only spy evil and ugliness, to have an ear that can be pleased by others' verses—yes, and by your own. Any one who thinks much of fame, and more of pelf than of fame, had better turn his attention to prose, for he will have ceased—supposing that he ever was one—to be a poet. Moreover, let no one expect to keep the necessary attributes much beyond youth. The few who do so have to " hark back " to their youthful experiences, in the description of which the acquired art comes in useful. But without these experiences and these memories they would have to retire. The season of love, the spring-time of life, is the season of poetry, and few are so fortunate—or unhappy, who can say ?—as to protract this season into old age. The young and talented envy such—they are very few—their grey beards.

Charles Collins is not even pointed out as the future Laureate. No one has anything to gain by the demonstration, as he is not a repayer of such coin. Yet he still writes and writes well. Sometimes he even converts poetry into prose ; but other people have already learnt the trick of this. There is nothing now-a-days of which the original patentee is long permitted to reap the sole profits. He soon becomes only a member of a firm. Charles Collins lives happily at Beddington, where he and Maggie are not likely to be separated from the old Squire till the latter leaves them for ever.

The original Poet—the once well-known Prothero Corthee—has, in the natural course of things, turned critic. At first, when he found himself unappreciated at home, he decided to cross the Channel, where he had no doubt that the poetic temperament of our neighbours would be enthusiastic in favour of what he still called his " Muse." He was received on his arrival with open arms, but, as he soon discovered, with more idea of ridiculing than of worshipping him. In fact, there were a considerable number of French poets—it is a mistake to imagine that England has a monopoly of unappreciated minor bards—who thought that any spare praise—to say nothing of profit—had better come their way than go to glorify or enrich a son of *perfide Albion.* Mr. Corthee had not been long in Paris striving to ingratiate himself with the McCawmee Joneses of his adopted country before an absurd parody of the poem which he considered would procure him immortality appeared in the *Figaro.* Immortality of this sort he did not desire, and indeed might have had without crossing the Channel. He packed his belongings as speedily as possible, and returned to the land of his birth with the less regret that he had discovered, on declaring his intention of becoming a French citizen, that he would have to serve in the French army. The discovery had an effect which was not surpassed by the experience of "the roughest passage on record" as he returned.

There was a good deal to be said in favour of his joining the ranks of the critics. He had "failed in literature," and of art he knew next to nothing. What could he do better than provide that others should fail too? He has lost his brush, and is naturally jealous of those who are growing or still keep the appendage. Few will complain that inferior or unsuccessful authors should eventuate into critics. It is surely better than that criticism should be written by those who have served no apprenticeship at all. The hedge-carpenter is on occasion preferable to none.

Mr. Jones, the original critic, has given up criticizing poetry. The minor bards, he said, were too jealous and too touchy. He writes a great deal, and better than ever, since matters of which he is entirely ignorant arise day by day less frequently. He never was a bad fellow at heart, and now as he gets older he is developing into a good one. By the time he is a hundred he will be as perfect as can be expected of a mere mortal, and it seems a pity that the improving process should in so many cases be deferred till the advent of middle age. He takes almost a paternal interest in the Collinses, and is vexed that one whom he never deposed has not done more with his opportunities. As he was godfather to her husband's first book, it is fitting that he should be godfather to Maggie's first boy. Of his duties in the latter position he probably knows almost as much as the majority of godfathers do now-a-days. Maggie and he are close friends, and he has never been known to show the least jealousy of the man whom he is still confident that he would have supplanted, if it had not been for the appearance of "that bothering white hat of Corthee's" at the garden door.

THE END.

Richard Clay & Sons, Limited, London & Bungay.

WARD AND DOWNEY'S
NEW BOOKS.

GOSSIP OF THE CENTURY : Personal and Traditional Memories. With more than 100 Portraits. By the Author of "Flemish Interiors." 2 vols. Royal 8vo, 1050 pp. 42*s.*

The *Athenæum* says : "It is better conceived and better arranged than nine-tenths of its class. . . . Its chapters are well arranged. It starts with a budget of 'Court Gossip,' chiefly about George IV. and William IV., and their surroundings. To this follows half a volume about social, literary, and political celebrities—and after that we have chapters on soldiers, lawyers, and doctors. The second volume is filled with reminiscences of musicians, singers, actors, and public entertainers in general—painters and sculptors being included in the category. . . . More than a hundred illustrations, most of them portraits and copies of old works, add much to the interest of these sumptuous volumes."

ANGELICA KAUFFMANN : a Biography. With a list of her Paintings and Drawings, and some Illustrative Repro-ductions thereof. By FRANCES A. GERARD. New Edition, crown 8vo. 6*s.*

The life story opens with an account of her childhood, 1741-1765, and is followed by a record of her girlhood, womanhood, middle and old age. The biography contains many letters, those in the late Prince Consort's collection being made use of. Help has also been obtained by Miss Gerard from Pro-fessor Gebhardt, Mrs. Ritchie, Messrs. William Rossetti, Alfred Morrison, Algernon Graves, Sidney Colvin, and others. The book, which is illustrated, gives a list of Angelica Kauffmann's paintings, and also of Bartolozzi's engravings after her pictures and designs (these number nearly a hundred), and of the houses she decorated.

SOCIAL ENGLAND from the Restoration to the Revolution. By W. C. SYDNEY, Author of "England and the English in the Eighteenth Century." 1 vol. 10*s.* 6*d.*

"He has an eye for what is picturesque, a taste for what is curious, and enough sense to divide his survey equitably between the scandals and follies of the town and the soberer life of the rest of England."—*Times.*

THE INSANITY OF GENIUS: and The General Inequality of Human Faculty Physiologically Considered. By J. F. NISBET, Author of "Marriage and Heredity." Third Edition. 1 vol. Crown 8vo. 6*s.*

"The book is a curious and interesting one."—*Times.*
"Open its pages where one will, one is confronted with matter of interest alike to the scientific inquirer and the mere seeker of entertainment."—*Saturday Review.*

ENGLAND AND THE ENGLISH IN THE EIGH-TEENTH CENTURY. By W. C. SYDNEY. 2 vols. Demy 8vo. 24*s.*

"Mr. Sydney has succeeded in picturing the men and women, costumes and pastimes, coffee-houses and clubs, vices, follies, and superstitions of the past century, in a highly graphic and realistic manner. . . . A useful and delightful book."—*Daily Telegraph.*

MEMOIRS OF DR. R. R. MADDEN. With Portrait.
Edited by R. More-Madden. Demy 8vo. 7s. 6d.

" His visits to many climes and cities of men, his literary tastes, and his friendship with Lady Blessington, Count D'Orsay, and a host of celebrities, furnish abundant material for a fascinating biography."—*Times.*

A CRUISE on the FRIESLAND BROADS. By the
Hon. Reginald Brougham. Illustrated. Demy 8vo. 3s. 6d.

" There is a delightful freshness about this thoroughly unconventional narrative."—*Land and Water.*

PICTURESQUE LONDON. By Percy Fitzgerald. With
upwards of 100 Illustrations. 25s.

" We are delighted to get a book like ' Picturesque London,' itself a triumph of the printer's art."—*St. James's Gazette.*

" It is all about the curiosities of London, the quaint old houses, and the odds and ends of archæology and street lore."—*Daily News.*

ANTHROPOLOGICAL STUDIES. By A. W. Buckland.
1 vol. Crown 8vo. 6s.

" Her object has been so to popularize her subject as to induce her readers to pursue the study for themselves, and if a pleasing literary style, and an admirable faculty of clear and lucid description are the essentials of success in that object, she may be assured that she will achieve it."—*Athenæum.*

'TWIXT OLD TIMES AND NEW. By the Baron de
Malortie. Demy 8vo. New Edition. 3s. 6d.

" Told with the spirit of the genuine story-teller."—*Saturday Review.*

" Crammed with incident and anecdote."—*Athenæum.*

IN LADIES' COMPANY ; Six Interesting Women. By
Mrs. Fenwick Miller. Fcap 8vo. 5s.

" Mrs. Miller has given us a volume to be grateful for."—*Daily Chronicle.*

" They are ample, suggestive, and neatly finished—turned off with true literary skill."—*Globe.*

TWO YEARS AMONG THE SAVAGES OF NEW
GUINEA : With Introductory Notes on North Queensland.
By W. D. Pitcairn, F.R.G.S. Crown 8vo. 5s.

" This is a capital work of travel. It records in an unpretentious fashion the experience of a couple of years on the coast of New Guinea and the neighbouring isles ; it narrates some thrilling adventures by sea and land ; and the author, without having much literary polish, has a happy knack of telling his story clearly and dramatically."—*Morning Post.*

ROBERT LOWE, VISCOUNT SHERBROOKE. By
J. F. Hogan, M.P., Author of "The Irish in Australia." 1 vol.
10s. 6d. A biography which mainly deals with Mr. Lowe's
life in Australia.

" Mr. Hogan has really rendered a great service to history and biography by his account of the very remarkable part played by Mr. Lowe in his colonial career."—Mr. Justin McCarthy in the *Pall Mall Gazette.*

SOLDIERS AT SEA. Illustrated. 2*s*. An account by a non-commissioned officer of the daily life and experiences of a battalion of soldiers ordered abroad.

TWO NEW BOOKS FOR CHILDREN.

THOSE MIDSUMMER FAIRIES. By THEODORA ELMSLIE, Author of "The Little Lady of Lavender." With 29 Illustrations. Crown 8vo. 6*s*.

"Will be a great favourite with many children. The book is daintily bound, and has some fine illustrations."—*St. James's Gazette.*

PIXIE. By Mrs. BLAGDEN, Author of "Trash," &c. With Illustrations by EDWIN J. ELLIS. Crown 8vo. 3*s*. 6*d*.

" It is very delightful reading for little ones."—*Daily Chronicle.*

THREE BOOKS ON HOUSEKEEPING.

FROM KITCHEN TO GARRET : Hints to Young House-holders. By Mrs. PANTON. New and Revised Edition (8th). Crown 8vo. 6*s*.

"A most useful and comprehensive book."—*Lady.*

NOOKS AND CORNERS. A Companion Book to " From Kitchen to Garret." By Mrs. PANTON. Crown 8vo. 6*s*.

"A veritable encyclopædia of useful information in all matters pertaining to the home."

LOVE IN A COTTAGE : or, Making the Most of a Small Income. By Mrs. HODGSON. 1*s*.

POEMS.

FATE IN ARCADIA, and other Poems. By E. J. ELLIS. With 24 Illustrations by the Author. 7*s*. 6*d*. Large Paper, with 10 additional Illustrations, 21*s*.

"The most striking poem, however, in the volume, is one that describes the survival of Christ's human nature after its Divine counterpart had returned to heaven. The theology is unsound, but the skill and the force with which Mr. Ellis has worked out his thoughts are unquestionable."—*Literary World.*

"'Eros' is a virile conception, strongly handled."—*Artist.*

" It might seem like a reflection upon Mr. Ellis's poetry to praise the designs with which he accompanies it, but such is not the case ; the illustra-tions are worthy of the verse, and that is saying much, for the verse is far above the average."—*Bookseller.*

" It is rare to come across a book where the poems have all been written obviously for the sake of the feelings and thoughts, where the verses seem to come out of a great depth of emotion which exists for itself alone, where every beautiful image and simile is but, as it were, the embroidered hem of the garment of reverie which wraps its author's life about."—*Bookman.*

IN A MUSIC-HALL, and other Poems. By JOHN DAVIDSON. Author of "Scaramouch in Naxos," "Perfervid." 5s.

"The section which gives its title to the volume is the most novel in the collection, and it is not wanting in daring. Obviously, it is the most open to diversity of opinion. It possesses at any rate this curious merit, that it demands re-perusal and yet again re-perusal."—*Academy.*

"It is clever, and certainly not tame."—*Review of Reviews.*

"Mr. Davidson's book is poetically graceful and morally courageous."—*Glasgow Herald.*

"His six sketches of music-hall 'artistes' are a little cynical perhaps, though they are undeniably clever. . . . Good poetry is always best left to speak for itself. Mr. Davidson's can well do that."—*Star.*

POEMS BY JOHN FRANCIS O'DONNELL. With a Biographical Sketch by RICHARD DOWLING. Crown 8vo. 5s.

"Poems very far above the average."—*Athenæum.*

BY FITS AND STARTS. By J. MORRIS-MOORE. 1 vol. 3s. 6d.

CHESS HANDBOOKS.

THE CHESS-PLAYER'S VADE MECUM AND GUIDE TO THE OPENINGS. By G. H. D. GOSSIP. 1s.

MODERN CHESS BRILLIANCES: A Collection of 75 of the most brilliant Chess masterpieces on record. By G. H. D. GOSSIP, Author of "Theory of Chess Openings," "The Chess-Player's Vade Mecum," &c. Crown 8vo. 1s.

NOVELS IN ONE VOLUME.

HOLY WEDLOCK. By C. T. C. JAMES, Author of Humbling His Pride." 6s.

"Mr. James has written a brilliant book. The story is a sort of Impressionist study of one side of modern life. The canvas is small, but the observation and accuracy with which it is painted are beyond all praise, and every character is made to lead up to the central idea."—*Saturday Review.*

THE INCOMPLETE ADVENTURER. By TIGHE HOPKINS, Author of "The Nugents of Carriconna." Crown 8vo.

"The hero is a delightful creation."—*Literary World.*

MISS EYON OF EYON COURT. By KATHERINE S. MACQUOID, Author of "At an Old Chateau," &c. Crown 8vo. 6s.

"A masterpiece."—*Pall Mall Gazette.*

MRS. GRUNDY AT HOME. By C. T. C. JAMES, Author of "Holy Wedlock." 6s.

IN FOOL'S PARADISE. By H. B. FINLAY KNIGHT.
Crown 8vo. 6s.
" Among the strongest of the one-volume novels which have lately appeared.
The faults are those common to a first work—a certain lavishness of good
things not necessary to the story, and a want of connection about the whole."
—*Daily News.*

MISS WENTWORTH'S IDEA. By W. E. NORRIS.
Crown 8vo. 3s. 6d.
" It is marked by a fine reserve, in the treatment alike of its tragedy and
comedy. The people whom we meet in its pages are life-like and well-bred."
—*Daily News.*

A BAFFLING QUEST. By RICHARD DOWLING, Author
of " An Isle of Surrey," &c. Crown 8vo. 3s. 6d.
" A story of singular interest and remarkable power."—*Scotsman.*
" Its interest, like that of ' The Moonstone' or ' Armadale,' is really enthralling. . . . It shows more power and finer quality than most books of its
kind."—*Speaker.*

DECK-CHAIR STORIES. By RICHARD PRYCE, Author
of " Just Impediment," &c. Crown 8vo. 3s. 6d.
" This is perhaps the most readable, and, in other respects, the most
remarkable collection of short stories that has been published this year."—
Academy.

KILMALLIE. By HENRY JOHNSTON, Author of " Chronicles
of Glenbuckie." New and Cheaper Edition. 3s. 6d.
" His two little volumes are real literature, and deserve to become classics."
— *Westminster Review.*
" Mr. Johnston works in a vein peculiarly rich ; from it he has already
produced some excellent material, and we expect much more from the same
quarter."—*Pall Mall Gazette.*

CAPTAIN LANAGAN'S DOG. By EDMUND DOWNEY
(F. M. ALLEN), Author of " Through Green Glasses," " The
Voyage of the Ark." 3s. 6d.
" This volume more than maintains the reputation its author has made."—
Star.

THE GREAT MEN AND A PRACTICAL NOVELIST.
By JOHN DAVIDSON, Author of " Perfervid." Crown 8vo.
3s. 6d.
" The stories are excellent, and the humour is very choice."—*Glasgow
Herald.*

THAT HATED SAXON. By the LADY GREVILLE (Lady
Violet Greville). Illustrated by E. J. ELLIS. With
Coloured Frontispiece. 7s. 6d.

THE LAND SMELLER, and other Yarns. By E. DOWNEY,
Author of " The Voyage of the Ark." 3s. 6d.
" A thoroughly interesting and amusing volume."—*Daily Chronicle.*

GEORGE WARING'S CHOICE. By FRANK BARON.
Crown 8vo. 6s.
" The character-drawing is skilful, the style good, and the story itself con-
vincing."—*Daily Chronicle.*
" ' George Waring's Choice' is vigorously written and faithfully realistic."
—*Morning Post.*
" It is a tale of intensely real life . . . The story is a good one, well
written, well worth reading, and very deeply interesting."—*Scotsman.*

NOVELS IN ONE VOLUME (Continued).

AN OCTAVE OF FRIENDS. By Mrs. LYNN LYNTON.
Crown 8vo. 6s.
"A decidedly entertaining collection of sketches and stories."—*Daily Telegraph.*

IN TWO MOODS. From the Russian 'of Korolenko. By
STEPNIAK and WILLIAM WESTALL. Crown 8vo. 6s.
"Full of power."—*Saturday Review.*

IN THE TILTYARD OF LIFE. By HENRY NEWALL.
Crown 8vo. 6s.
". . . Some of the stories are distinctly good."—*Athenæum.*
"The last tale, 'A Jew in Moscow,' is well and forcibly written, and from what we know of the treatment of the Jews in Russia it might be thought to be founded on fact, so strange is the fiction."—*Publishers' Circular.*

BEN CLOUGH. By WILLIAM WESTALL. Crown 8vo. 6s.
"The book will be eagerly read by all who take it up."—*Scotsman.*

A FLUTTERED DOVECOTE. A New Humorous Novel.
By GEORGE MANVILLE FENN. With Sixty Illustrations by
GORDON BROWNE. Crown 8vo. 5s.
"Mr. Fenn shows in this story a positively Pickwickian humour."— *Spectator.*

ARCHIE CAREW. By J. FRANCIS, Author of "The Story
of Mary Herries." Crown 8vo. 6s.

THE STORY OF THE LIFE OF JÖRGEN JÖRGENSON.

THE CONVICT KING. With Reproductions of Original
Drawings by JÖRGEN JÖRGENSON. By J. F. HOGAN, Author
of "The Lost Explorer." Post 8vo. 2s. 6d.
"We can cordially commend this book to young and old; they will find it interesting, amusing, and instructive."—*Athenæum.*

PERFERVID : The Career of Ninian Jamieson. By JOHN
DAVIDSON. Illustrated by HARRY FURNISS. 2s. 6d.
"For those who can enjoy the absolutely grotesque, a prose extravaganza, somewhat in the Gilbertian style, the career of Ninian Jamieson will provide a good deal of amusement."—*Athenæum.*

BRAYHARD : The Strange Adventures of One Ass and
Seven Champions. By F. M. ALLEN. Illustrated by HARRY
FURNISS. 2s. 6d.
"Brimful of jokes, repartees, and comic situations. . . . It is absolutely delicious."—*Guardian.*

DARRELL'S DREAM. By C. HORNER. Crown 8vo. 3s. 6d.
". . . A readable volume . . . of startling incidents and miraculous coincidences, with one of those wonderful visions thrown in which interest the Society for Psychical Research."—*Times.*

COSETTE. By Mrs. MACQUOID. Crown 8vo. 3s. 6d.
"Few can rival Mrs. Macquoid in her stories of Continental life, and 'Cosette' will rank among the sweetest of her most delicately-painted sketches."—*Figaro.*

FORTHCOMING BOOKS.

OUR VIANDS: an Historical Account of Staple Foods. By A. W. BUCKLAND, Author of "Anthropological Studies." 6s. [*March.*

THE GHOST WORLD. By J. THISELTON DYER, Author of "Church Lore Gleanings." 1 vol., 10s. 6d. [*April.*

VARIA: The Smallest Church in England (Greensted, Essex)— Benvenuto Cellini—Childhood's Drama—Samuel Pepys, &c. By JOHN ASHTON, Author of "Social England under the Regency." With numerous Illustrations. 1 vol. demy 8vo, 10s. 6d. [*May.*

SOCIAL STUDIES. By Lady WILDE, Author of "Ancient Legends of Ireland," "Notes on Men, Women, and Books." 1 vol. 6s. [*May.*

THE LIFE AND CAREER OF MOLTKE, with an Examination of the Strategy of the Campaigns of 1866 and 1870. Two Portraits, Maps and Plans of the principal Battlefields. By His Honour Judge MORRIS. £1 1s. [*June.*

CRIME AND CRIMINALS IN AUSTRALIA, with Descriptions of some Notorious Gangs of Bushrangers. By H. A. WHITE, Governor of Ballarat Gaol. 6s. [*August.*

THE DEVIL IN BRITAIN AND AMERICA. By JOHN ASHTON, Author of "Social England under the Regency." With numerous Illustrations. 1 vol., £1 1s. [*August.*

CURIOUS TALES OF THE BANK OF ENGLAND. Illustrated. 1s. [*Shortly.*

WHEN A WOMAN'S SINGLE: the Experiences of a Governess. By M. EASTWOOD. 1s. [*Shortly.*

A NEW BOOK OF PROVERBS. By the Author of "Lazy Thoughts of a Lazy Girl." 1s. [*Shortly.*

POEMS CHIEFLY AGAINST PESSIMISM. By J. S. FLETCHER. 3s. 6d. [*March.*

NEW AND FORTHCOMING NOVELS AT 2s.

IN PICTORIAL COVERS.

GRIF. By B. L. FARJEON. New Edition.

GREAT PORTER SQUARE. By B. L. FARJEON. New Edition.

THE SPANISH GALLEON. By F. C. BADRICK.

ANCHOR WATCH YARNS. By E. DOWNEY.

KING OF THE CASTLE. By G. M. FENN.

PRINCESS SUNSHINE. By Mrs. RIDDELL.

SAPPHIRA. By SARAH TYTLER.

THE BEECHCOMBERS. By G. BISHOP.

EIGHT BELLS. By HUME NISBET.

THE LAND OF THE HIBISCUS BLOSSOM. By HUME NISBET.

ROY'S REPENTANCE. By ADELINE SERGEANT.

FORTHCOMING NOVELS IN THREE & TWO VOLUMES.

A SECRET OF THE PAST. By VICTOR O'D. POWER, Author of "Bonnie Dunraven." 3 vols. *[March.*

TWO MEN AND A WOMAN. By Mrs. GEORGE BISHOP. 2 vols. *[March.*

MICHELINE. By HECTOR MALOT; Translated by JULIA RAE. 2 vols. *[April.*

A PASSAGE THROUGH BOHEMIA. By FLORENCE WARDEN, Author of "The House on the Marsh," &c. 3 vols. *[April.*

BY RIGHT OF SUCCESSION. By ESMÉ STUART, Author of "One for the Other," &c. 3 vols. *[May.*

THE EMU'S HEAD. By W. C. DAWE, Author of "Mount Desolation." 2 vols. *[May.*

JUANITA. By J. FOGERTY, Author of "The Countess Irene," "Mr. Jocko," &c. 3 vols. *[June.*

AN ACTRESS'S LOVE STORY. By MABEL COLLINS, Author of "The Prettiest Woman in Warsaw," &c. 3 vols. *[June.*

ONE NEVER KNOWS. By C. F. PHILIPS, Author of "As in a Looking Glass," "Constance," &c. 3 vols. *[July.*

IVY AND MYRTLE. By JOHN BRIDGES, Author of "A Brummagem Baron," &c. 2 vols. *[July.*

FORTHCOMING NOVELS IN ONE VOLUME.

BY A HIMALAYAN LAKE. By An Indian Exile. Crown 8vo. 3s. 6d. *[March.*

MR. JOCKO. By J. FOGERTY, Author of "Countess Irene," &c. With Illustrations. A New Edition. 6s. *[March.*

POETS ALL. By JOHN BRIDGES, Author of "A Brummagem Baron," &c. Crown 8vo. 3s. 6d. *[April.*

THE ARTISTIC TEMPERAMENT. By CHARLES H. BROOKFIELD. Crown 8vo. 3s. 6d. *[April.*

BAPTIST LAKE. By JOHN DAVIDSON, Author of "Perfervid," "The Great Men," &c. Crown 8vo. 3s. 6d. *May.*

THE HEART OF TIPPERARY. By W. P. RYAN. With an Introduction by WM. O'BRIEN, ESQ., M.P. Crown 8vo. 6s. *[May.*

AN UNCO STRAVAIG. By COCHRANE MORRIS, with Illustrations by the Author. 5s. *[June.*

GLADDIE'S SWEETHEART. By THEODORA ELMSLIE, Author of "Those Midsummer Fairies." 3s. 6d.

WITH THE HELP OF THE ANGELS. By WILFRED WOOLLAM. 3s. 6d.

THE TUC-UN-UNUN-DI LODE. By "Australian Native." 6s.

AT THE GATE OF THE FOLD. By J. S. FLETCHER, Author of "When Charles the First was King." 3s. 6d.

WARD & DOWNEY, 12 YORK ST., COVENT GARDEN, W.C.

www.ingramcontent.com/pod-product-compliance
Lightning Source LLC
Chambersburg PA
CBHW031402270326
41929CB00010BA/1296